I0101124

The Proper Care and Feeding of Singles

How Pastors, Marrieds, and Church Leaders Effectively Support Solo Members

R.M. Buchanan

Pix-N-Pens Publishing
The Proper Care and Feeding of Singles

ISBN-13: 978-1-944120-50-4
ISBN-10: 1-944120-50-5
E-book ISBN-13: 978-1-944120-51-1

Published by Pix-N-Pens Publishing;
PO Box 702852;
Dallas, TX 75370

Learn more about author Ruth Buchanan at her blog: www.ruthette.blogspot.com or at her author page on WriteIntegrity.com.

Printed in the United States of America.
Library of Congress Control Number: 2017955555

TABLE OF CONTENTS

DEDICATION

For (and because of) Port St. Lucie Bible Church: pastors, elders, deacons, members, and friends.

Thank you. I love you.

> Now that I think back, being single in the church was a very discouraging time for me.
> ~ Rebecca, Married

INTRODUCTION

This is an important topic. The best proof is the excitement with which single Christians chipped in with interviews, information, and advice. They basically fell over themselves to share my survey with their pastors, church leaders, and married friends. All of them agreed that this book matters.

WHY DOES THIS BOOK MATTER?

MOST CHURCHED SINGLES ARE DISSATISFIED WITH THEIR EXPERIENCES IN CHURCH

The data collected uncovers significant levels of concern, confusion, and discomfort regarding the place of the single Christian in the modern evangelical church. Almost without fail, the Christian singles I interviewed welcomed this project with open arms, expressing their nearly-universal delight over the concept and requesting that I send their pastors a copy—this before I'd even set a single word to page.

THE CHURCH IS NOT DOING AS WELL AS IT THINKS

Evidence from the data indicates a surprising divergence of opinion between what married members and church leaders think they're communicating versus what the singles are actually picking up. Whether this is an issue of what's being communicated or how it's being received, the data indicates that most congregations experience a gap between expectations and reality. Most pastors and leaders believe that they're doing a good job ministering to singles, but many singles expressed some level of dissatisfaction. Even if this is a simple communication issue, it is worth addressing.

The Situation Seems to be Spiraling

As Millennials come of age within the church, marriage rates continue to decline.[1] At the same time, the Barna Group reports that even while the younger generation is backing away from marriage (or at least delaying marriage significantly), meaningful relationships still remain one of the main reasons that Millennials will stay connected to the church.[2] The church, therefore, must learn how to foster meaningful relationships or risk hemorrhaging a steady stream of disconnected young singles into the world. If pastors hope to change the Millennial generation's low view of marriage and family, they must keep the Millennials in church long enough to influence them. This will be accomplished not by pandering to them but by understanding what drives their decisions and seeking to bridge the gap.

The Resources Are Lopsided

Christian bookstores teem with resources to deepen ministry to almost every group in the Church, marginal or otherwise: children, teens, tweens, combat veterans, retirees, ethnic minorities, the mentally and physically disabled, and married couples—*especially* married couples. Marriage-strengthening is a huge focus of Christian resources, as well it should be. I do not begrudge the marrieds their need for specific scriptural counsel. Even so, it seems that everyone gets focused spiritual-growth for their lifestyle circumstances (or stages) except the singles. To me, this seemed more of an oversight than anything else at first, but the lack of research and resources focusing on singles in the local Church tells a different story.

There are books on Christian singleness, yes; but many are books *about singleness* written *by singles, for singles*. They're all more or less helpful, but only to a point. Because these books are marketed to the singles themselves, the messages don't reach beyond their target demographic. Perhaps a further step is required.

Even in the professional and semi-professional blogosphere, there seems to be little available by way of helping Christians prepare for a life of singleness other than telling singles to

1) stay sexually pure, and
2) either learn to be content with singleness or resign themselves to spiritual failure.

Living the single Christian life is more nuanced than that, and our message must reflect that understanding.

Where are the resources to help church leaders and marrieds address the specific spiritual, relational, and emotional needs of their single Christian friends? What would those resources look like? What would they say? How would we use them? This project seeks to lay the groundwork for answering some of these questions.

Before we move forward, however, we must establish some foundational expectations.

WHAT YOU CAN EXPECT FROM THIS BOOK

This Book Won't Advocate for Singleness Over Marriage

The union of marriage is part of God's plan to reveal Himself to the world, and God cares about families because He patterned the family after the mystery of Christ (Ephesians 5); therefore, the question is not how to promote the concept of Christian singleness over marriage.[3] Instead, this book will focus on how best to minister to the singles in your church.

As the world drifts further and further from the biblical moorings of sexual ethics, the way in which the Church takes marriage and family seriously will make a clear statement about who we are and what we represent.[4] However, with society as a whole trending away from the nuclear family—for good or for ill—singleness issues will become increasingly critical to navigate as the Church moves forward.

This Book Will Offer Data Analysis

Over a nine-month period, I surveyed hundreds of singles, marrieds, and church leaders concerning perceptions of singleness issues in local churches. I asked all three groups the same sets of questions; then I compared their responses to see how well perception on the part of marrieds and leaders stacked up with what singles claim to experience. Although responses are totally subjective, the clear divide warrants attention. I will highlight areas of divergence and recommend how these differences can be resolved into unity.

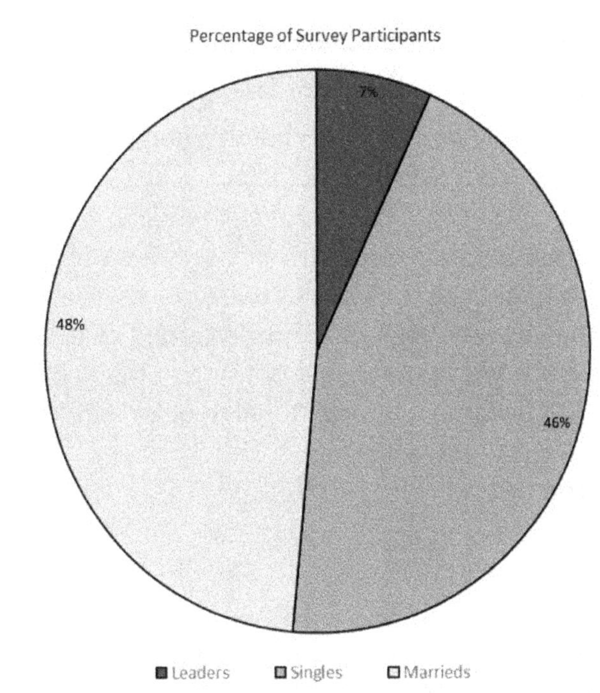

*Some Leaders also classified themselves as Single/Married, creating slight overlap.

This Book Will Offer a Peek into the Psyche of the Christian Single

Through personal anecdotes and stories collected from my own life and hundreds of Christian singles of all ages and backgrounds, I will present a composite sketch of how it feels to live as a single in the Church: the good, the bad, and the awkward.

This Book Will Offer Tips for Better Friendships and More Effective Soul Care

The way recent data trends, churches will likely see an increase in their population of singles in the days to come. The time has come to ask if the singles in your church are being effectively shepherded, encouraged, spiritually challenged, and used in the areas of their giftedness in accordance with the Scriptures and to the best of your church's ability.

This is not a topic that I have put a great deal of thought into over the years. Even if none of [my] answers are useful, it was a good exercise to at least think about these things. We are always looking for better ways to reach a wider group of people, both with the Gospel and discipleship. It is a step in the right direction as Paul said, to become all things to all people, that I might win some.
~ Jerrill, Married/Pastor

I've been to one church where I felt valued as a single and one where it was all about marrieds and families. The leadership sets the pace.
~ Anonymous, Single

Hope you can shed some light on how we can better serve the needs of this special group of brothers and sisters in Christ. By the way, I have this guy I would like to set you up with. He would be perfect for you!
~ Sarah, Married

Note: On rare occasions, comments from survey participants have been slightly edited for clarity.

CHAPTER 1

I SEE SINGLE PEOPLE

Statistics demonstrate that we have more single people in North America now than ever before. According to the 2010 United States Census, 43% of all residents age eighteen or older are single. Of that group, 61% have never married. Not only are fewer Americans marrying than in previous generations, but the ones who do wed are marrying at increasing ages.[1] According to the Pew Research Center, only 26% of Millennials between the ages of eighteen and thirty-two have married, as opposed to 36% of Gen-Xers, 48% of Boomers, and 65% of the Silent Generation. While the men of the 1950s married around the age of twenty and the women at twenty-three, Millennials tend to marry at the respective ages of twenty-seven and twenty-nine.[2]

This trend doesn't seem likely to reverse anytime soon, and the reasons behind the shift are complex. Some Millennials have chosen to delay marriage for economic reasons. They may want to start off their marriage and family life at the same level of comfort their parents provided for them. Recent research also builds an interesting case that many single men and women today actually delay marriage not because they necessarily *want* to, but because they suffer from an over-abundance of choice. Instead of choosing from a limited (mostly geographically-based) pool of potential suitors in the way that their parents and grandparents did, the current generation finds itself faced with a nearly limitless set of options through social media, web-based dating sites, and the high mobility opportunities of modern culture. Rather than making it easier for men and women to find one another, the sheer volume of options paralyzes singles.[3]

To understand this principle in action, allow me to offer a hypothetical scenario. Let's say that you're in the market to adopt a puppy, and I have volunteered to help you. In due time, I turn up at your house with three adorable puppies. I say you are free to adopt whichever one you like best. You may, of course, decide that none of the three puppies works for you; but no matter which option you choose, the process is fairly straightforward.

> Married and single people have very similar needs, and I think one of the worst things the church does is treat them like they're each a different species. With a little bit of thoughtfulness, it's possible to provide ministries that attend to the specific needs of people in different life situations (I hate to even say "stages" as it seems to encourage the view of singles as "proto-marrieds") without artificially dividing the Body of Christ where it isn't necessary.
>
> ~Jonathan, Married

Now imagine that instead of showing up with puppies, I sit you down at a computer and pull up a web page with an entire grid of pet adoption photos. At the bottom of the page, you see little, numbered boxes, [1], [2], [3], [4], and so forth, indicating that you have many pages of options to sort through. Along the side of the screen is a text box advertising *other* sites with *other* pages of *other* potential choices. Even if you saw a likely adoption prospect on the first screen, wouldn't you feel that, given the many options available to you, there's probably a better puppy out there, if only you invested enough time to find the right one?

Though puppy adoption and dating aren't exactly the same thing, the parallels are undeniable. With a seemingly limitless array of connections available through social media and dating websites, why shouldn't singles take as much time as they want to search through every possibility to see which one is best? Perhaps this could be the reason why despite having more ways to connect with potential spouses than ever before, today's men and women looking toward marriage have their own difficulties in finding a life partner.

Some singles, of course, have decided to opt out of marriage entirely. Many who grew up in homes affected by divorce find the idea of marriage doesn't hold much charm. Other singles suspect that with overall social conventions trending away from marriage, there seems to be no need to marry in order to build their lives on biblical foundations.[4]

Because of the high value the church places on marriage, the statistics of never-marrying and late-marrying singles inside the church won't always march in lockstep with the statistics taken from general society. There's a simple reason. Since its inception, the church has valued the institution of marriage highly, and it is fully appropriate that this is so. Marriage and family are part of God's natural design for humankind. They act as a stabilizing force in the world and, more importantly, serve as a living metaphor of the union between Christ and the Church.

Exact statistics on percentages of married versus single congregants proved difficult to find due to a lack of research in this area. But while there may seem to be more singles outside the church than within it, if you open your eyes and give the Sunday morning crowd a hard look, you'll probably find more singles than you expected.

OPENING YOUR EYES TO THE SINGLES

Opening your eyes to the singles in your church starts with a definition of the term *single*. If you equate *single* with *unmarried young adult*, then you're already a step behind.[5] Singles in the church can be sorted into five groups.

FIVE GROUPS OF SINGLES IN THE CHURCH

Group One: Never-Married Singles

The Never-Marrieds most likely make up the largest portion of your church's single population. Because of that, they get the most attention when it comes to singleness issues[6] (that will also be true in this book). These Never-Marrieds have remained single for a variety of reasons, but if pressed to tell you why they haven't married, they will be at a loss for what to say. Many wanted to marry long before now, but somehow the process stalled. Others are single because they thought they'd found a good match, but something went wrong: now here they are, still single at a certain age.

Increasingly, young singles are deciding to delay marriage in favor of personal freedom. They use their twenties to travel, study, and focus on their careers. A few will stay single forever: whether by the call of God, their own personal choice, or the personal choice of every other single person on the planet.

Although the Never-Marrieds are the majority within the minority, don't forget that they're still a minority in the church. Even the Never-Marrieds who are satisfied with life can feel out of step with their married peers. Many lack sufficient community, intimacy, and accountability. Helping them become fully integrated into the Body is vital, and not just for their sake. In God's plan for His church, we all need one another.

Group Two: Divorced Singles

No matter the reason behind their divorces, many Divorced Singles equate the failure of their marriages with the failure of their faith. Unfortunately, instead of offering sympathy and support to their divorced friends, fellow brothers and sisters in Christ sometimes offer an extra dose of judgment.

Divorced Singles fear that regardless of how the divorce came about—even if it was against their will—they'll forever be treated as spiritually second-class, at permanent fault for failing in one of Christianity's primary cultural undertakings. Sometimes this feeling is just a perceived one; other times it's real. Either way, it must be overcome. Be sure it's not something that can be said of your church. Divorced Christians already feel alienated and forgotten, both in social situations and ministry opportunities. Divorced parents with children need extra support—both practically and emotionally. They should not be needlessly sidelined from the work of the Body or the ministry in which they excel. The Church needs the voices of brothers and sisters who have experienced this particular pain. Men and women who have been carried through the pain of divorce in the Lord's strength find themselves in a better position to counsel, comfort, and support others who suffer deep loss. As Elizabeth Elliot reminds us, "In God's management of the affairs of men suffering is never senseless."[7]

> In my last church, which was very family-focused, I often felt like being divorced and childless put me at the bottom of the ladder of personal value. A divorced woman with children is treated much better than one without, because at least she's fulfilled the cultural mandate.
>
> ~ Brenda, Single.
>
> 
>
> I was once in a Sunday School class where someone made the statement, "I don't understand people taking the easy way out and getting a divorce." Among my divorce-recovery friends were two former ministers' wives whose husbands had initiated the divorce, a former minister's wife who had been physically abused by him, and a woman whose husband decided to change sex. To say divorce is an easy way out is a slap in the face—probably in the majority of cases. Churches need to be aware of the gut-wrenching pain—not the looseness of morals or lack of effort on the part of single-agains.
>
> ~ Anonymous, Single
>
> 
>
> Sometimes, it's not the person's choice to divorce. Never look down on single parents, definitely not before you know their whole story. I'm so tired of feeling like a second-class citizen. It makes me not want to go to church sometimes.
>
> ~ Anonymous, Single

Group Three: Widowed Singles

After the death of a spouse, Widowed Singles must adjust to a new normal. Depending on how long they were married, they might actually need to re-learn how to live alone. Once the initial outpouring of love and support in the immediate aftermath dries up, Widowed Singles must continue living day-in, day-out without the warmth and comfort of the spouses they had learned to rely on. The grief cycle is different for everyone, but most bereaved spouses find that they need more support than people remember to give.

Widowed Singles may feel pressured to remarry before they are ready, or they may seek to remarry more quickly than their friends, family, former in-laws, or church family are prepared to see. Either way, they suspect that their choices are bound to upset someone. Most Widowed Singles aren't sure how to navigate their new situations. As 1 Timothy 5 acknowledges, the particular situations of widows may vary; and the church family bears a responsibility to acquaint themselves with the individual needs. In turn, the church benefits from their godly Christian service.

> I'm a widow, so I have experienced both sides. I wish there was more taught about showing respect and compassion regarding singleness and parenthood. I find it perpetually amazing and baffling that people seem to think two of the biggest life decisions one can make—who to spend your life with and whether or not to have kids—are somehow free game for discussion and questioning. I know many people who heartbreakingly long either to be married or to have kids or both. Yet so many people are oblivious that there is even a possibility that this is a sore spot or that they should test the waters a bit before diving right in.
>
> ~ Anonymous, Single

GROUP FOUR: THE FUNCTIONALLY SINGLE

No matter the reason for the separation, Functionally Singles operate alone within the Body of Christ. These members may be living apart geographically from their spouses due to career, estrangement, or military service. They may be married to partners who are absent in church life due to unbelief or spiritual regression. Whatever the reason, when it comes to church life, Functionally Singles are alone. They come alone, sit alone, negotiate ministry opportunities alone, and perhaps even wrangle kids without the consistent help of another adult. If your church divides Bible study classes based on marital status, Functionally Singles find themselves in an awkward position. They can't attend the singles class; yet if they attend the marrieds' class, the question becomes, "So, where's your husband/wife?"

> Though it may be difficult to attend church alone, do it and find ways to get involved. Being involved helps you to be part of something larger than yourself—a church family. That family can be a help and support.
> ~ Traci, Married

Because the Functionally Single doesn't fit neatly into any one category, knowing how best to help members of this group can be a challenge. Each one might have very specific relational, emotional, and spiritual needs. While their situations might differ, they may be just as lonely as other groups of singles; yet because they aren't technically "single," their relational needs aren't recognized as such. Please don't overlook them. Their unique experiences can offer the church fresh perspectives on love, life, community, and ministry.

Group Five: Older Singles

Whether single by choice, widowhood, or divorce, Older Singles have distinctly different needs from younger ones. Their struggles to connect to the church body are vastly different from the other groups in this list. No matter the origin of their singleness, these Older Singles must be thought of in a different category entirely, and their needs considered as such. They're often lonely and needing support, and many of them have wisdom stored up to share with those who would reach out. They need you, and you need them.

> As an older single, the difficulties are distinctly different than as a young single... It seems even harder to connect with people in church. They like you and are friendly at church functions but you don't fit into day to day activities or holidays. If you want to connect you have to initiate and host. That can be exhausting.
> ~ Debby, Single

AWARENESS

Now that you're mentally acquainted with the five primary groups of singles in the church, you'll start seeing single people everywhere you go. Much like Haley Joel Osment whispering the source of his own personal torment to Bruce Willis in *The Sixth Sense*, you will soon find yourself leaning forward in the pew, wide-eyed, informing fellow church members in your own special pseudo-creepy whisper: "*I see single people!*"[8]

Single people are not creepy, but it's good to raise awareness of their existence. For a group that attests to feeling overlooked fairly consistently, awareness could be half the battle.

SEEING THE NEEDS

Awareness is a great first step, but how do you best serve these singles once you've learned to spot them? How well do you understand the unique emotional, relational, and spiritual needs of your single friends?

To uncover the answer, I formed a survey designed to address this very question. I solicited input from hundreds of believers from all over the country, asking singles how well they felt that their married friends and church leaders understood them, while simultaneously asking marrieds and church leaders how well they understand their single friends. Although the responses are totally subjective, I found data comparison quite enlightening. I hope you do, too.

THE MARRIEDS

When asked how well they understood the struggles of their single friends, married respondents admitted that they probably don't get it right all the time. While many of them stated that they do try, they admitted there's probably room for growth.

- "I remember from when I was single. However, in some ways, I feel disconnected from that point in my life. I also feel there are some aspects to life now that add more pressure to singles that I didn't deal with."
- "I *think* I can anticipate most of [singles' needs], but I don't get how they trouble most singles people, and I can honestly say that I don't have time to worry about them."
- "When I was single, social media wasn't a thing, so I don't think I fully understand being single in this society."

- "I think by simply considering this an issue, I am ahead of many married individuals in terms of understanding the challenges of being single."
- "I have a good enough memory to remember how disenfranchised and diminished I sometimes felt as a single. I try to keep that in mind."
- "I hated the angst and uncertainty of being single."
- "I could tick off a list of things I think they probably experience, but I would not be speaking from a place of deep understanding."

On the whole, the tone from the marrieds was encouraging. They seemed invested in reaching out to their single friends more effectively and hinted that they could probably do better with further guidance. Reading their responses gave me great hope.

PASTORS AND CHURCH LEADERS

Pastors and church leaders seemed even more optimistic about their ability to empathize with singles and minister to their needs. This makes sense, given that most married respondents had little actual ministry training and therefore felt ill-equipped to claim any sort of expertise. Pastors and leaders, however, with their specialized training, feel more prepared to tackle the issue head-on. When asked if they understood spiritual and relational needs of long-term singles, most of the pastors and leaders gave thoughtful, constructive responses.

- "I have some idea [of what their needs are]. I ask [Singles] questions for their unique view of their relational status. There are many shades of singles."

- "[I understand] poorly; however, empathy is a constant challenge as with most minorities (widows/widowers, the elderly, the poor, the destitute, etc.). You do not need to personally experience every life circumstance to Scripturally minister to people."
- "I understand spiritually, yes. Their spiritual needs would inherently be no different than the married person. Relationally? No."
- "Singles have some needs in common with [others], but they are not all from the same cookie cutter. Some of their needs coincide with the needs of married people in their age group. The main thing we must remember is that everyone needs a personal relationship with the Lord. As ministers, we are to lead singles (and others) into a meaningful relationship with Him."
- "Although I think I understand the issues of being lonely or having their biological clocks ticking, I would be foolish to say that I completely understand what a single person is going through."
- "I need a definition of terms. Single can mean retirement age with your mate deceased or divorced and single or never married. All are singles, but all may have a slightly different perspective. I have a single 93-year-old father, a single 83-year-old mother-in-law, a divorced and single 42-year-old daughter, and a single, never-married 35-year-old young lady in our church. So, I'd like to think I have a fair understanding of the challenges."

By and large, I found the responses of pastors and church leaders warm, hopeful, humble, and supportive. Pastors and elders cited Scriptural reasons behind their approaches, and even when their opinions diverged, I could see that they'd given the questions serious, biblical consideration.

Such responses brought me to question this book's major premise. I began to question whether or not pastors and church leaders actually *needed* a book to guide them in effectively shepherding their flocks' solo members. If the care singles were receiving in most churches matched the responses these pastors gave, I could thank God and move my attention elsewhere.

Then I calculated the data and took a look at the numbers.

THE NUMBERS

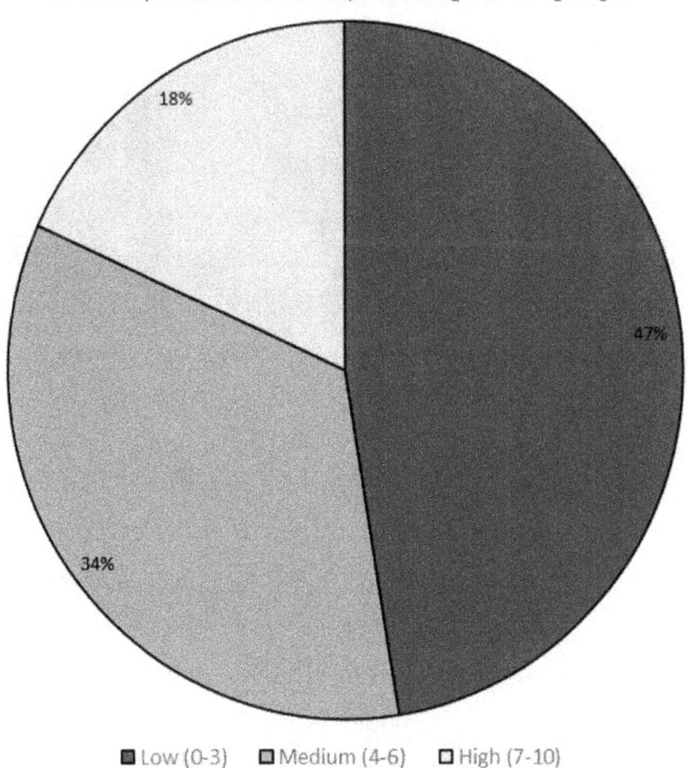

On the surface, these numbers don't look so bad. Although nearly half of the singles give their married friends and church leadership fairly low marks, a full 18% gave these same groups very high marks. The question, however, isn't just how singles rate their married friends and church leaders, but in how the church leaders and marrieds perceive their effectiveness in the same area. When all three groups' numbers are seen side-by-side, an interesting trend emerges.

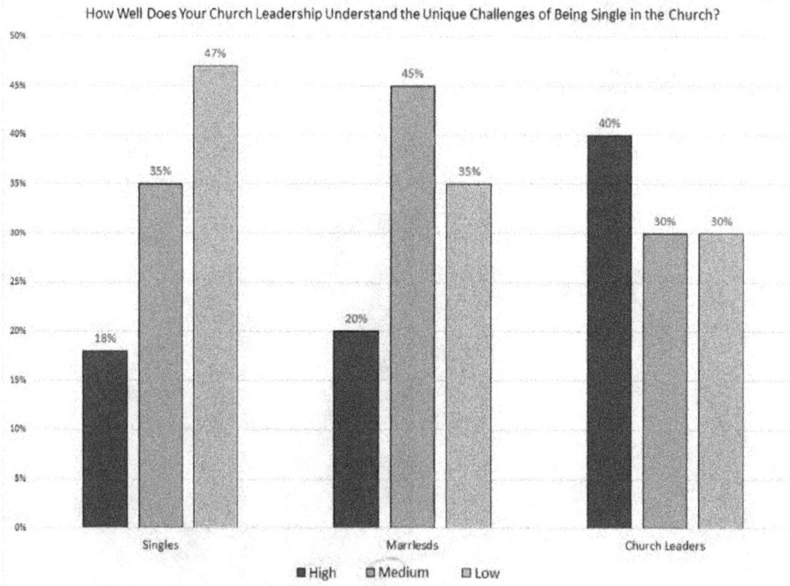

Although these results are not what we would like to see, at least the married folk anticipated their low rankings: only 20% claimed a good understanding of singleness issues, with the rest admitting a measure of ignorance.

The real surprise came from church leaders, most of whom self-reported a high level of understanding: 40% felt confident that they understood singleness issues very well (10% actually rated themselves as a 9 out of 10 on the sliding scale). Yet the singles do not perceive the effects of this knowledge.

This divergence could be due to one of the following root causes: that church leaders unconsciously lack a grounded understanding of singleness issues, they have not been effective in communicating that understanding to the singles under their care, or the singles have incorrectly perceived their leaders' efforts on their behalf.

Clearly, something's off. As I contemplate that high number on the church leadership side, I cannot help but remember some specific comments made by singles who took the survey. When asked what they think their respective church leaders think about singleness, here's what some of them said. Although the way in which some of them express themselves may seem off-putting initially, bear with them. Their sentiments are worth noting.

- "[Leaders] obviously understand it because they were single once. But they've forgotten, so they still end up making boneheaded remarks that show surprising ignorance. But usually, once you explain it to them, they're like, 'Oh, right. Of course.'"
- "I think most of them think that being single is a problem."
- "I think they quickly forget how easy it is to stop involving single people in your social life once you are married."
- "I think being single and a man is much more acceptable than being single as a woman. She may be considered a spinster while he is considered a catch."
- "They understand what it's like to be human and a

Christian, but I often feel like we're from different universes."

- "[My leaders] are good men who try to be what their congregation needs. I think it's just so far off their radar that they've never even thought of it."
- "In thirty years of church-going, I don't *ever* remember a sermon or lesson or devotional specifically addressing singleness. On the other hand, there have been many, many times where a sermon about marriage had tacked on the end, 'Of course, single people can learn from this too…'"
- "I feel that sometimes they forget. They try, but they forget."
- "I feel like there are conflicting messages in the church. We should obviously be content with what God has for us, but we should also be honest with sharing our desires with God. I want to be persistent in my prayer life without being whiny. It's a struggle."

Woven like a refrain through the survey responses was the singles' overwhelming assumption that their pastors and leaders view them as abnormal because they are unmarried. This issue cannot go unaddressed.

THERE IS NO NORMAL

Marriage is normative for the Christian experience. The Bible clearly advocates for marriage; therefore, pastors are right to encourage biblical marriage among their church members. However, if this pro-marriage message is somehow interpreted by the singles as "If you are not married, *you* are not normal," a communication breakdown occurs. This is likely wholly unintentional on the part of the speaker; however, the message that single people aren't normal, although generally inadvertent, provides a prime opportunity for a root of bitterness, especially in the hearts of singles who desire marriage.

We must pause to remind ourselves that within the bounds of the human experience, there really is no normal. You have never seen a "normal" human. I don't mean that in a jokey, we're-all-a-little-weird way, either. We've never seen normal humanity because we've never seen sinless humanity. We're all wrecked by sin, fallen from our intended state: married, single—all of us. There is no "normal" on this earth, and there hasn't been since Jesus' feet lifted from the Mount of Olives.[9]

Marriage may be the expected *status quo* within the church, but it is not the ultimate vision of what it means to be a Christian. We may learn certain aspects of Christlikeness through the service and self-sacrifice of the marriage covenant, but marriage is not life's end goal.

The end goal of Christianity is total restoration and reconciliation with God through the finished work of Jesus. Through His sacrifice on the Cross, Christ made all reconciliation possible—God to man, man to God, male to female, and married to single.

The world will never again see this perfection until our Lord makes all things new—and we eagerly anticipate that day—but we're still left with some challenges right now.

THE PROBLEMS AT HAND

Pastors and church leaders claim a high level of understanding for the problems facing the singles in their congregations, yet the singles perceive a lack of empathy. If that lack is indeed present, one of the following factors may lie at the root:

Leaders haven't considered the question in detail

This is understandable. No matter what positions church leaders hold, they're swamped—senior pastors especially. Having grown up with a senior pastor for a father, I witnessed this dynamic firsthand. Most pastors and elders do try to see issues from every angle so as to expound the Word effectively to their members. Like Paul, they want to become "all things to all men" (I Corinthians 9:19-23). However, in many churches, married couples and families are the most dominant demographic. As such, their situations are more likely to be immediately recognizable, known, and understood.

Leaders have considered the question, but believe that a focus on singleness issues is moot—if not counterproductive to unity.

I had a lot of long talks with pastors regarding this very question, and it will be addressed fully in a subsequent chapter. For now, I will clarify that I'm not advocating for attention to singleness issues *over* the issues of any other group. The ultimate goal of this book is to strengthen the bonds of unity within the Body, not to cause further divisions.

Leaders put more trust in their own memories of being single than they should

Although currently-marrieds had their own times of singleness, for many of them, these experiences took place long ago. The social and cultural landscape has shifted considerably since the currently-married Boomers and Gen X-ers were single—in a big way. In addition, although their experiences as a single may have felt long at the time, many of these leaders were only single through their early twenties, which is very different from being single long-term.

AN ALTERNATIVE ASSESSMENT

While the perceived lack of empathy might be rooted in one of the issues detailed above, it could also result from a general lack of communication. If the only time your singles are addressed directly from the pulpit are in throwaway comments tacked on to a sermon on biblical marriage, or if the only time the singles hear from you is when you need something from them (such as volunteering for childcare or coming early to an event "because it's easier for you to be on time for things since you won't be trying to get your kids ready,") then of course they will react poorly. At best, they'll feel used. At worst, they'll feel disenfranchised and resentful.

Singles should be valued as children of the King who have been crafted in the image of Christ just like other believers. They are unique members with distinct spiritual gifts and skill sets. Singles of all ages and backgrounds need to be seen, known, and loved—not as a group, "The Singles," but as individuals with personally specific needs, hopes, dreams, and fears. They need to be spiritually challenged—not to become better spouses someday, but to become better suited as the Bride of Christ. This will only happen as they're fully integrated into the church body.

Any steps taken to address this concern will be unique to your church, but there's no denying that at least for now, many churches are missing the mark.

Hence this book.

A WAY TO THINK ABOUT THE PROBLEM

More than anything else, problems seem to arise from false assumptions on both sides. Every church scenario will be different, of course, but most survey responses indicated that while pastors, marrieds, and leaders seemed to think they were doing fairly well responding to singles' needs, singles assumed that their needs were given very little thought. Unless marrieds, singles, and church leaders agree to come together in mutual respect and

> The biggest problem is the lack of a connection or even encouragement in single life.
> ~ Anonymous, Single
>
> 
>
> "I wish people would start saying, 'You are valuable to this Body of Christ, and here's how,' and have what they say not be the fact that I watch their children. I wish people would say, 'You are totally worthy of being married. Wow, you would be a great mom and wife, but we are so thankful that God has you single right now, and here's why.' I wish marrieds in the church would ask me, 'What does your single life look like? I'm interested.' I wish older singles would share lessons they've learned without me having to pull and yank it out. I wish church leadership would ask and counsel without me having to initiate the conversation every time."
> ~ Beth, Single

understanding, communication glitches based on false assumptions will continue.

Remember, false assumptions don't have to be *wrong* assumptions in order to be false. That is, sometimes we use perfectly sound logic and good judgment to reason all the way to the wrong conclusion. Let's say, for example, I ask you to work a geometry problem. You must find the measure of the third angle in a triangle if the first two angles measure 45 degrees each. Since we know that within triangles, the sum of the three angles will always equal 180 degrees, then the third angle must be a right angle—that is, an angle measuring 90 degrees.

At this point, many of you are ready to give 90 degrees as your final answer. Perhaps you're also making a mental note to e-mail your high school geometry teacher to apologize for what you said about how you'd never use those formulas again "in real life." The rest of you, the more cautious ones, are waiting for the catch.

Because of course there's a catch.

What I failed to tell you was that the triangle in question was not drawn on a flat sheet of notebook paper but was instead doodled on the side of a soccer ball. You began the problem while operating under the assumption that you could use the formula you memorized in high school—the formula assuming flat-planed Euclidian geometry. However, because the lines of the triangle are bent by the spherical shape of the ball, you would actually have to practice non-Euclidian geometry.[10]

I didn't tell you the information you needed to solve the problem. That was wrong of me. Maybe I thought you might ask, but maybe you don't know enough about geometry to know that a question like that even *needed* to be asked. There's the rub. Of course, it's wrong for singles to withhold the information that you need in order to best serve them. It's also wrong not to ask the necessary questions to gather the information.

What if you don't even know the questions to ask?

Read on.

Discussion Questions:

1) How aware am I of the five groups of singles in the church: the Never-Marrieds, the Divorced, the Widowed, the Functionally Single, and the Older Singles? Can I name any of them among acquaintances?

2) How might the emotional, relational, and spiritual needs of a single person be different from those of a married person?

3) How can I more effectively reach out and befriend the singles that I know?

Action Points:

- Ask the Holy Spirit to open your eyes to the specific needs of the singles around you.
- Initiate friendship with a single.
- Ask specific questions regarding your single friends' needs. Do what's in your power to meet them if you can.

> Searching for a new church home as a single person adds a whole new dimension to the awkward relationship between the church and my single self!
> ~ Robby, Single

CHAPTER 2

WAY TO MAKE IT AWKWARD

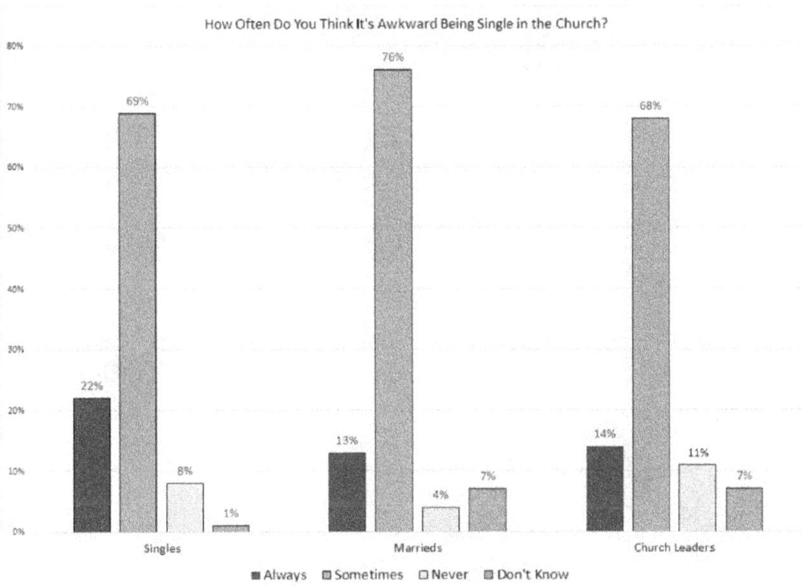

THE NUMBERS

Although I could have received more specific survey data if I'd allowed for the responses of *rarely* or *hardly ever,* I was more interested to see how many people, if given a narrow array of options, would opt for the extreme answers of *never* and *always*. (I'm also very interested to know why 1% of the singles surveyed apparently "don't know" whether or not it's awkward being single in the church. To these singles I say on behalf of all of us: We have questions.)

Although there's some slight variation, all three groups more or less agreed that sometimes it's awkward to be single in the church. Of course, it is. Sometimes it's awkward to do almost anything. Why bother writing a chapter addressing the problem if the problem has already been acknowledged? Because if we all seem to be equally aware of the awkwardness problem, we should all work equally to eliminate it. Unfortunately, this awkwardness is rarely addressed.

THE AWKWARD PROBLEM

One Sunday, while away from my home church, I ran into some people who knew my parents. A man I'd never met before instigated the following dialogue, he half-shouting the whole time (possibly due to hearing loss):

MAN: ARE YOU DOUG AND TINA'S DAUGHTER?
ME: Yes.
MAN: ARE YOU MARRIED?
ME: No.
MAN: WELL... GET MARRIED!
ME: Okay.
MAN: YOUR MOM WANTS GRANDKIDS!
ME: My mom already has nine grandkids.
MAN: WELL, SHE WANTS MORE!
ME: Okay.

That was our whole conversation.

It should be noted that this question would have driven some singles to weeping, wailing, and gnashing of teeth—especially singles who earnestly desire to marry or have recently suffered romantic disappointment. Fortunately for this man, I don't embarrass easily, nor am I surprised anymore by this sort of behavior.

Why did this man feel comfortable walking up to me, a virtual stranger, and making pointed comments about my personal life in front of God and everybody? Would this man have approached an unknown young married woman to make loud-voiced comments about her marriage?

Maybe he would have. But you know what I'm getting at. At least, I hope you do. My single friends know what I'm talking about. We all have some version of that story.

> I wish that people in my church would stop being so awkward about people being single. I've heard them ask me and my sisters about potential relationships, and before we could answer, immediately trying to backtrack, saying that, "it all will happen in due time." I really do not know what's going to happen to me, but the older couples from my church make marriage seem nebulous and yet inevitable, in a way that comes across as a little frightening.
>
> ~ Janiece, Single

OPEN SEASON ON SINGLES

For some reason, it's always open season on singles. I don't know why, but it seems that because we're not married, others feel great freedom to ask deeply personal questions while we're surrounded by an audience.

Even if these people are strangers. *Especially* if they're strangers. It's nearly always unsettling, but we've found that if we betray even a hint of frustration or annoyance during these public spectacles, we come across as defensive and are labeled as Bitter Singles. The general consensus seems to be that if we're going to be single past our twenties, the least we can do is be gracious about it (even though the source of our frustration in that moment is most likely not our singleness but in having been called out in front of a group).

When people find out that I'm in my late thirties and not married, they generally launch into a specific series of questions:

- You're not *married?*
- *Why* aren't you married?
- Did you ever *want* to be married?
- Do you think you ever *will* get married?
- What's wrong with all these guys?

Those aren't easy questions to answer (especially the last one, which I'll tackle in more detail later). Besides that, it's hard to imagine a world in which, when I meet new married friends, I immediately start grilling them on their personal choices.

- You're *married?*
- *Why* are you married?
- Do you *want* to be married?
- Do you think you'll *stay* married?
- What was wrong with all the other people you *could* have married, but didn't?

I certainly wouldn't ask such questions the first time we meet, especially not in front of an audience. So why does this happen so often to singles?

> I'm constantly getting questioned about my love life from church members. No one ever asks the married church members how their love lives are going.
> ~ Taylor, Single
>
> 
>
> I know many people who heartbreakingly long either to be married or to have kids or both. Yet many people are oblivious to the possibility that this is a sore spot or that they should test the waters a bit before diving right in.
> ~ Anonymous, Single

THE QUESTION OF AWKWARDNESS

As I read through the surveys, I discovered that the question of awkwardness was a sticking point for some church leaders. They were careful to remind me that some people are awkward in their own right. The church can't be blamed for this reality.

This is a fair assessment and one that hits close to home. I don't like to boast, but I can make almost any situation awkward. Let me assure you, however, that feeling awkward at church applies to singles in a special way, regardless of their own inherent awkwardness.

TOP SIX WAYS IT'S AWKWARD TO BE SINGLE AT CHURCH

When We Don't Have a Built-in Sidekick

The problem of not having a permanent partner manifests itself in several areas. First, visiting a new church always feels less intimidating when you're not alone. At least you have someone with whom to exchange significant side-eyes when the deacons light something on fire or the pastor pulls out snakes. Singles don't have this sort of emotional and physical backup. They face every new church visit alone, walking in with no human safety net.

When We Can't Decide Where to Sit

I'm the type of person who will plop down next to almost anyone. I've discovered through the interview process, however, that I'm somewhat of an anomaly. Many singles I talked to (especially women) feel awkward sitting alone at church, yet they don't feel comfortable foisting themselves on just anyone. It sounds like such a trivial concern; yet to some singles, it's a genuine struggle. Sitting alone in a sea of couples and families can lead to weekly bouts of emotional fallout.

> Many of my difficulties are of my own making because I am useless at introducing myself and plonking myself on to people.
> ~ Pam, Single

When We're Confronted with an Ingrained Couples Mindset

We live in a partnered world, and singles consistently throw off the numbers. After many years of attending work dinners, church socials, and other formal events alone, I considered taking dates—not because I felt social or emotional pressure to do so, but *just so that I wouldn't throw off the seating*. The small, round tables favored at these functions are invariably set up with an even number of seats and place settings, designed to hold no extras. I had three choices: I could seek out another single ahead of time to partner up for seating purposes; I could sit wherever I wanted, knowing I would eventually split up a couple who planned to sit together; or I could drag a chair and place setting away from another table and squish it in somewhere else, cutting down on everyone else's elbow room and genuinely annoying the event organizers. I understand this is a minor inconvenience, but it was a pretty consistent one, and it eventually irritated me so much that I contemplated taking a date just to escape the seating debacle; however, that didn't seem a good enough reason to ask friends to endure the tedium of an event to which they had no personal connection. (Besides, fake dates are generally more trouble than they're worth. Unless you happen to be starring in a romantic comedy—which, sadly, I never am.)

When We Can't Find a Class to Join

When churches offer their Bible-study electives based solely on marital status or life stages (College and Career, Young Marrieds, etc.), certain singles experience a special brand of tension. Middle-aged singles especially find themselves in an awkward spot. They've aged out of the College and Career group, but they're still too young for the retirement crowd. They're not Young Marrieds, and there's no class titled Oddly-Aged Misfits. Not that singles are misfits, but that's how they can feel when classes are structured in such a way as to exclude their unique situations. In that respect, the Functionally Singles also struggle, since they're caught somewhere in the middle.

When People Say Weird Things

Although I already touched on this topic in the chapter introduction, I'd like to treat you to what a few single survey respondents said when asked this question: "Is there anything that you wish people would stop saying to you or asking you?" For your entertainment, I've also included any commentary the survey-taker thought to offer.

- "Why are you still single?" I realize this [is] usually supposed to be a compliment, but really, exactly how many people know why they are still single? That question just makes me feel like there is something wrong with me.
- "If I were only twenty years younger…" And if I had absolutely no choice in the matter…
- Just this past weekend, while at a church retreat with the youth of the church, another student leader who was making a noble attempt to get to know me asked me about my age and marital/dating status. His follow up to my answers were consoling in nature— something similar to "I didn't get married until I was in my early thirties. And I know someone who didn't marry until his late thirties and he and his wife had a child later in life." He meant well, but the underlying message seemed to be "Don't worry. There's still time for you to reach normalcy."
- "Stop being so picky." Ummm, I'm going to be married to this person for life—how can I have a low bar for criteria?
- "Your feelings for her will grow." As if being married and forcing love to happen is somehow better than being happily single.
- "At this point, the good ones are all taken, so you've got to accept that any girls you meet are gonna have a kid or two that you have to deal with."
- "God has someone for you." Please show me in the

Bible where it says that.

- “Why is a handsome, good guy like you who loves Jesus still single?”
- “Don’t give up hope.” [This said] as if I don’t have *great* hope in my life, in a God who is magnificent and has eternal plans for my good.
- I don’t like it when people say, “It’s okay you are single. Singleness is a gift.” I understand what they are trying to say. But I don’t feel it is a gift for me. I desire to be married.
- "Don't look for someone because he should find you." If I didn't pursue/seek out opportunities to get to know my [current] boyfriend, we wouldn't even be friends right now.
- “You and [Insert Name] should date!”
- [People] come up to me and apologize that I’m still single. I might not even have been thinking about it if they hadn’t made that comment.
- “You need to go out there and find love.”
- “You really should not have such high standards. You're going to run out of time to have babies.” That's always so helpful and uplifting.
- Offering the "reason" of why I may still be single is not helpful and takes away the idea that it is in God's providential and sovereign care.
- I wish people would realize that when they say "you need a boyfriend/husband" or "why don't you have a boyfriend/husband?" they are, in essence, saying, "You, as an individual, are not enough" and/or "Why have you not managed to accomplish this basic life status?"

- "Just hang in there!" Like I have any choice?

For singles, the challenge lies in knowing how to respond to comments like these. For most of us, the scriptural admonition to speak the truth in love has rarely been more challenging.[1] Most singles know people mean well and are trying to encourage, but after a while, trying to respond to half-baked comments wears us down. Yet if we push back even a little, we could become labeled as "sensitive" about our singleness.

Recently, I talked with a woman who had made some inadvertently hurtful comments about marriage and singleness. Her immediate reaction was to fold her arms and say, "Well, I know never to talk to *you* about singleness ever again!" From my perspective, we'd been having a calm and reasonable talk, and her reaction was the exact opposite of what I'd hoped to accomplish. I didn't want to shut down communication; I wanted to expand it—to deepen its substance.

Fearing ruptures like these, we singles tend to nod and smile even when we're baffled. In that case, however, such reactions only serve as tacit approval, deepening the misconception that these statements are not only appropriate but also appreciated. Thus, the ongoing struggle.

When Someone's Fixated on Setting Us Up Whether We Like It or Not

I'll give advice on successful set-ups in a subsequent chapter. For now, just know that unless we're actively seeking set-ups, we find it awkward to fend them off without seeming ungrateful or defensive.

HOW YOU CAN MAKE THE CHURCH EXPERIENCE LESS AWKWARD FOR SINGLES

The church experience doesn't have to be awkward for singles—at least, not as awkward as some people insist on making it. You can be part of the solution by taking active steps toward making the singleness experience less awkward for everyone. Well, to the best of your ability. You can only do so much. The rest of the responsibility, of course, rests squarely on the backs of the singles themselves.

Be Sensitive to the Relational Dynamic

When new singles visit your church, be aware that for many of them, the simple act of showing up without backup displays courage, especially if they're from unchurched backgrounds. If you have a trained staff of greeters, chat with them about how they can better facilitate seating single visitors near church members especially attuned to this dynamic.

Singles report that when they visit a new church, they sometimes meet people who are not sure what to do or say when they encounter a single person, particularly when that single person is beyond what's currently considered the standard marriageable age. Said my friend Robby, "They aren't sure how to follow up their initial 'Are you here with your wife and family?' question because I imagine it's pretty rare that they hear a man in his late 20's or early 30's say that he's single and never been married." Unfortunately, people who aren't sure what to say when faced with an older single usually don't let their uncertainty stop them from making some sort of comment.

The good news is that they don't need to know what to say.

The fact that we're single doesn't need to be explained. It's merely a statement of fact.

Take the Initiative

Invite singles to sit with your family. Do this especially if they're new to the fellowship and have no connections in the church. Do this consistently, until the single feels that the invitation is open and that sitting with you every week is a given. If singles ignore your invitation multiple times, however, you can feel free to issue one last blanket invitation and move on. After all, there might be a reason they choose not to sit with you. At least you can say you tried.

Evaluate Your Programs

How deeply steeped in the couples mindset are your church programs? Churches are formed largely of couples and families, and most people in the church marry at some point. It only makes sense to arrange the flow of your events to balance to the majority. Family retreats, Valentine's socials, and marriage classes needn't necessarily cease. However, if your extracurricular programs consist *only* of such events, you may unwittingly alienate your singles. (If your response is to point out that you don't have many singles in your fellowship, ask yourself if there might be a reason.)

If you can make small tweaks to accommodate singles and show consideration to them whenever you can, they will love you for your thoughtfulness. Better still, they'll feel more tightly woven into the fabric of the church body.

Assess Your Approach

Happily, many churches have already stepped away from the

highly-programmed models favored in the 80s and 90s, when there was a slot for everyone based on age group: Children's programs, Teen Zones, College and Career, Young Marrieds, Mid-Lifers, and Autumn Leaves (or, as the senior group at my own church called themselves for a short time, the Pace Makers). Favoring community over programs seems wise for many reasons; however, since I don't aspire to write a work of profound ecclesiology, I won't probe too deeply here. For now, I will simply say that if you run a highly-programmed ministry that pigeonholes singles because of marital status alone, you've written a recipe ripe for resentment.

> Singles often resent being treated like a herd, even when advocates mean well. The needs, desires and expectations of singles are as vastly different as the needs, desires and expectations of married couples (think newly married versus a couple homeschooling eight kids!). As a pastor, I want to learn to lead with my ears, listening to the unique challenges and desires of people, single and married.
>
> ~ Peter, Married/Pastor

Personally, although I love my younger single friends, I find that I quickly grow weary of the larger-than-life emotions and unceasing energy. Being lumped in with fresh-faced college graduates just because we're all still single would make me feel old and tired (although I do appreciate their help with understanding current slang terms). Fortunately, my church has never really run a singles ministry, *per se*, and I've been free to connect with fellow believers of all ages, marital statuses, and genders. This is, after all, how it should be: older discipling the younger, younger energizing the older; singles helping marrieds,

marrieds helping singles—and so forth. This doesn't negate the benefits of occasional separated activities. However, interconnected church life is best fostered through a communal approach rather than a compartmentalized one.

Modify Your Comments

This won't apply to all readers, but perhaps it's time to modify your approach to commenting on singles' personal lives. Stop asking invasive questions in front of strangers. Stop joking about their marital status if you're not close enough to know how they feel about the situation. Stop offering blanket life advice without context. Stop assuming that you know how they feel about the possibility of marriage and family, especially if you haven't invested time in getting to know them individually. Bear in mind that when you make such comments, church life feels harder for singles than it needs to be.

Ask Before Acting

> I try to take all advice as [if] a concerned person is trying to be helpful and may not understand my whole story. I try to smile and be gracious.
> –Vana, Single.

If you're thinking of setting up singles, remember to ask them first. Really, it's that simple. If they say they're not interested, move on. If they say yes, proceed with wisdom and discretion. If the pairing works out, rejoice. If it doesn't, don't push. Remember, two wholly awesome people won't be compatible just because you want them to be.

A FINAL WORD ON AWKWARDNESS

It is true that some people are plain awkward. Others will find fault with whatever the church does or take up irrational offense over truly innocent comments. We must, however, resist the temptation to fall back on these loopholes to dismiss the whole problem. The point of this chapter is not how to help single people learn to be less awkward—the awkward ones will need to read a different sort of book. The point of the chapter is to highlight problem areas noted by the majority of the singles consulted and to offer active steps that your church can take to provide a warm welcome and an emotionally-nurturing environment for singles.

> "Oh, you're single and she's single, therefore you should get together!" As if having a pulse qualifies us being compatible.
> ~ Anonymous, Single
>
> 
>
> I've really only set up one couple for dating, and they have been married for ten years.
> ~ Linda, Married
>
> 
>
> I set a friend up once when I was still a very young married person. They did not appreciate it at all. It was super awkward for everyone, and I wanted to die.

Yes, some singles have difficult personalities. Some imagine slights were no slight is intended. Some will be grumpy sad sacks no matter what. But remember that when Paul encouraged the Thessalonian church to comfort the fainthearted, he did not follow this with a note that the fainthearted stop being so sensitive.[2] Paul likewise reminded the Romans that they had an obligation to support the weak without lecturing the weak regarding their need to gain strength.[3]

No matter what church we attend, we're certain to be surrounded by flawed people, but their flaws do not give us license to treat them however we wish or use their weaknesses to excuse ourselves from responsibility. Within the Body of Christ, the strong are called upon to minister to the weak, not to look down on them for their weaknesses.

In many respects, the church is the visual representation of our theology. Within the Body of Christ, we manifest, on a small scale, the coming Kingdom of God.[4] Through the preaching of the Word we are convicted and comforted. Through community, we give and receive love, counsel, edification, encouragement, mercy, and grace. Through outreach and service, we spread the gospel both implicitly and explicitly.

This is our purpose. It is important work.

If any specific, thoughtful actions on our part can make church life more effective, should we not prayerfully consider taking those steps?

Discussion Questions:

1. In what situations have I witnessed the "Open Season on Singles" dynamic at play in my church family? What can I do to address these situations in a biblical way?
2. What can our church do to mitigate awkwardness for single visitors?

Action Points:

- Issue a standing invitation for a single to sit with your family during church services and at other events.
- Try being involved in at least one church activity apart from your identity as a couple. You'll be surprised at how showing up solo opens your awareness to what your single brothers and sisters experience.

CHAPTER 3

TACKED ON

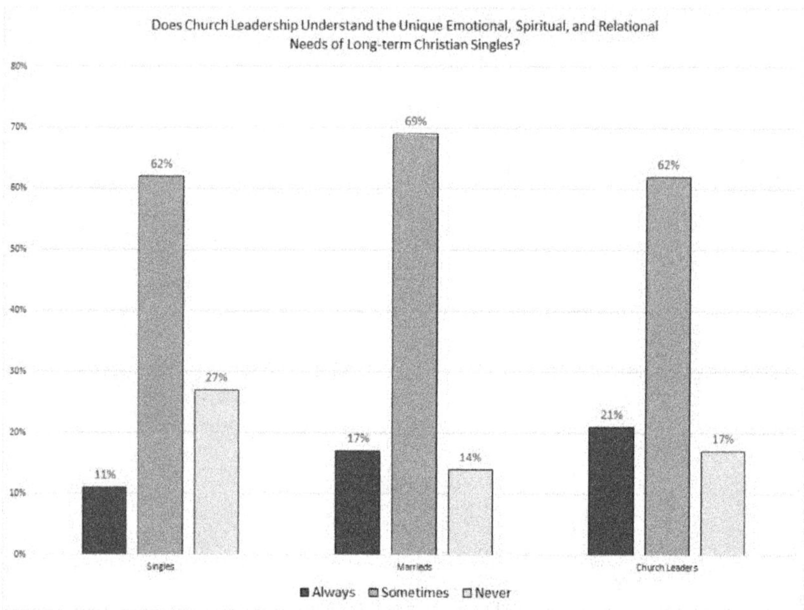

When I first started surveying pastors, I was shocked by how many of them told me flat-out that they do not take into consideration the unique needs of singles while fulfilling their responsibilities in the church. When I designed the question, I fully expected 100% of them to say that they 100% considered everyone's point of view.

Had the pastors who answered *No* somehow misunderstood the question? Had the ones who answered *Sometimes* at least offered some perspective in the comment section? When my own pastor answered *No*, I almost fell off my chair. My pastor—who's proven himself mindful of the single condition, even offering thoughtful commentary from the pulpit from time to time—said he doesn't consider the needs of singles. Surely, I'd phrased the question wrong, or the pastors had misunderstood it, or my data-collection service had fritzed.

To track down a solution, I followed up with some of these pastors. I'm so glad I did. The more questions I asked, the more complex our discussions became. Then I realized some of my survey questions could have been more specific. However, given my current lack of time travel abilities, I'll use the gathered data to help shape the discussion. Thanks to some help from my pastor friends, we all have a chance to view this data through clearer lenses.

> I don't know if I've ever heard a sermon or a lesson about singleness. At least not without also hearing that singleness is just a preparation for marriage. Or to hear the complete opposite: that some people are called to be single. I want to ask, what about those of us who want to be married and find themselves adrift at the moment because we're not, and we don't know how to change that situation?
> ~ Sarah, Single

WHAT THE PASTORS SAID

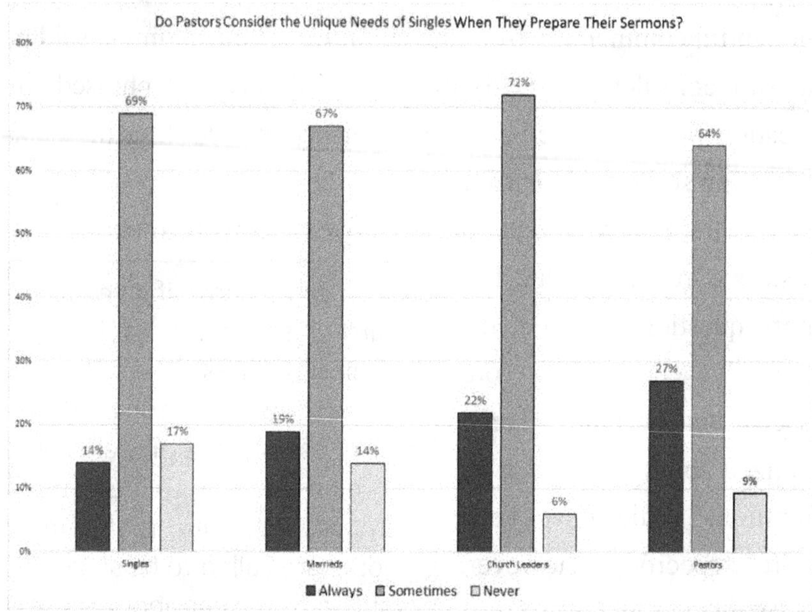

Pastors bear the responsibility of entire congregations. Although a pastor's approach to personal counseling may center on individuals and their specific problems, the ministry of preaching is meant to be over-arching. When the Word is ministered effectively, the Spirit of God applies specific truths to individual hearts as He wills. By and large, pastors don't consider it their responsibility to "preach at" specific people (or groups of people) from the pulpit unless a given text warrants it.

That's why systematic expository preaching through the entire Bible is so vital. Studying and preaching Scripture in its fullness ensures that pastors teach the whole counsel of God, leaving no issues by the wayside—including the specific truths that would benefit singles.

As Tim Keller explains, expository preaching lets the text set the agenda and keeps preachers from adapting messages too much to their preference or their own pet issues. In this way, expository preaching keeps ministers of the Word from focusing too keenly on issues that occupy most of their own personal thoughts and attention and facilitates attentiveness to all areas of spiritual life.[1]

Expository preaching will also help congregants develop a strong understanding of systematic theology, which in turn fuels their personal exegesis. Eventually, this pattern develops into a synergistic feedback loop, strengthening the biblical foundation of the whole Body. That's why, as Kevin DeYoung says:

> Good systematic theology will be anchored in good exegesis. The sum of the whole is only as true as the individual parts. No Christian should be interested in constructing a big theological system that grows out of a shallow and misinformed understanding of the smaller individual passages. I don't know of any evangelical pastor or scholar who disagrees with these sentiments.[2]

Unfortunately, this process isn't borne out in every church. Seminary president Al Mohler laments that over the last few centuries, theology has somehow transformed in people's minds as something reserved for academics and professors rather than average pastors and church-goers like themselves.[3] Because biblical theology is now divorced from daily life for many Christians, they are less equipped than ever to recognize what's happening when their pastors fail to preach God's truth—or, even worse, go completely off the rails.

When pastors serve congregations a steady diet of topical sermons lacking strong theological underpinnings and broad biblical context, the results are far from fruitful. Church members are hindered in developing a strong foundation in systematic theology, and often only the felt needs of the loudest majority are addressed. Should we be surprised that within such a framework, Christian singles feel forgotten and devalued?

> For the most part, pastors speak to the majority. If the majority of their adults are married, that's what they're going to focus on. They just call us singles out during the sermons for the 'when you get to this point in your life' points.
>
> ~ Tamber, Single

There's also something to be said for how a pastor's conversation partners shape sermon preparation. This concept is laid out clearly by Timothy Keller in his book on preaching—a book so good that I'd love to repeat it in its entirety right here, but apparently, that would violate copyright law. For now, I will just offer this:

> [Sermon] application will naturally rise from your conversation partners. If you spend most of your time reading instead of with people, you will apply the Bible text to the authors of the books you read (which is fairly unhelpful). If you spend most of your time in Christian meetings or in the evangelical subculture, your sermons will apply the Bible text to the needs of evangelicals (which is far more helpful but still incomplete). The only way beyond this limitation is to deliberately diversify your people contact.[4]

Sermon preparation accomplished in the office is important, but it's not the only element shaping the message. Fellowship, discipleship, and friendship are valuable not only in their own rights but also as vital elements forming sermon preparation. If you do not maintain streams of godly dialogue with the singles in your church, how will you hope to stay in tune with their spiritual struggles? This isn't just true of singles, of course, but of every person with a walk of life differing from your own.

GETTING IT RIGHT

Based on survey comments, singles are annoyed that the only time they're mentioned from the pulpit is when they're tacked on to a sermon centering on marriage or family issues, i.e.: "You'd better listen up, singles! Your turn is coming!" If you give the matter some thought, you'll quickly understand why. There are actually several serious problems with this sort of rhetoric.

> I don't think most people look outside of their experiences, and that is a detriment to the church.
> ~ Becca, Married

The first problem is that comments like these don't even apply to all of your singles. The next time you're tempted to say something like this, think of an eighty-one-year-old widow staring up at you over the rim of her glasses.

The second problem is that these comments aren't theologically sound. Every person will *not* marry one day. Some singles will answer calls of service and celibacy, foregoing earthly family for the furtherance of the Gospel and the Kingdom. Others will long for marriage their whole lives but will still die unwed. We live, after all, in a broken world.

By calling out singles in this way, you've likely only distracted them from your message. Instead of enticing them to listen to your points, you've most likely sparked a furious inner monologue refuting your comments.

Therefore, rather than falling back on the unconvincing (and often inapplicable) "you might need this someday" line, consider giving the singles in your congregation a more compelling reason to listen. God didn't include anything in Scripture because we *might* need it *someday.* We *all* need it *all*—now.

The Sunday before I began drafting this chapter, the text for the day at my church was I John 2:12-14:

> I am writing to you, little children, because your sins are forgiven for his name's sake.
> I am writing to you, fathers, because you know him who is from the beginning.
> I am writing to you, young men, because you have overcome the evil one.
> I write to you, children, because you know the Father.
> I write to you, fathers, because you know him who is from the beginning.
> I write to you, young men, because you are strong, and the word of God abides in you, and you have overcome the evil one.

Hearing the family-relationship words in the passage, perhaps some of the singles or childless in the congregation may have been tempted to tap out mentally, assuming that since they're not raising children, the passage need not apply to them. They would have been wrong.

For a full understanding, this passage must be read in light of the context. The Apostle John uses family-relationship words throughout his short epistles, often referring to his readers as "little children." He saw the readers as children because he considered himself their spiritual father.

One of my pastor's points on the text was as follows:

> *Spiritual* reproduction is our goal. Scripture assures us that you can be single or childless and be [equally] as spiritual as anyone else. The Apostle Paul and Timothy proved that. Who won more spiritual children to faith than Paul? No one that we know of. [Marriage] is not a [criterion] of spirituality. The church does not have family dynasties like the Kennedys and the Rockefellers. You don't see that. What you see are spiritual children.[5]

This point is well taken, and no one gets cut any slack. It's fully possible that in following the biblical mandate to be fruitful and multiply, some parents are shirking their spiritual responsibilities of nurturing their children spiritually and bringing them up in the Word. Instead, they delegate these tasks to youth group leaders and Sunday School teachers. It's also likely that the unmarried and childless among the congregation routinely ignore the biblical mandate to produce spiritual children by winning souls and mentoring believers who are physically or spiritually younger than themselves. This passage calls hearers of all marital statuses to focus on what really matters: our responsibility to contribute to the spiritual formation of those within our own circles of influence. The core teaching allows no wiggle room for anyone. Both singles and marrieds must confront this doctrine of discipling head-on and assess how their choices line up with its challenge.

When a pastor friend of mine pre-read an early draft of this chapter, he asked why more singles don't recognize the huge impact they could have through mentoring spiritual children. I can't answer for the rest of the singles, but I can say that in all my years of attending church multiple times per week and listening to many weekly radio-broadcast and podcasted sermons, I don't remember hearing direct, clearly-articulated calls for singles to consider this ministry. Singles are often admonished to devote themselves to service and chastity, but most calls to service are general rather than specific. I'm not sure why this concept is so often overlooked, because it's a huge focus of the New Testament, both in prescriptive passages and in observable relationships (Jesus and his disciples, Paul and Timothy, and so forth).

I think most singles would be thrilled with more of these specific sermon applications and less of the garden-variety "wait-your-turn-is-coming" stuff. Not just because we want it, either—we need it.

Just as the deepest need of married people is not to strengthen their marriages, likewise the deepest need of unmarried people is not to prepare for marriage or find a spouse. The deepest need of every human heart is to be confronted with the cross of Christ.

Only when we've bowed the knee can our lives be shaped by the hands of the One who bore the nails. As we are conformed to His image, we will bring glory to our Creator, be it through strong marriages or sanctified single living. Only the Holy Spirit makes such a transformation possible. Good preaching helps.

When the Word of God is wielded by the Spirit of God through the person of God, needs are always met. We would all benefit greatly if this process were played out weekly in churches around the world; however, in many churches, this just isn't the case. Many of us can identify with John Piper's lament in his book *The Supremacy of God in Preaching:* "One reason why people sometimes doubt the abiding value of God-centered preaching is because they have never heard any."[6]

Let that not be said of us!

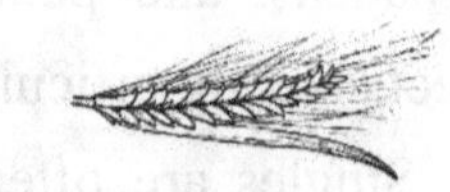

Discussion Questions:

1. What examples have I heard of singleness issues being tacked on to a sermon about marriage and family?
2. Why is it so important that singles are given specific scriptural calls to mentor spiritual children?

Action Points:

- Incarnate Christ to a single this week by offering sacrificial love, care, help, and concern.
- Make a single in your life the focus of dedicated prayer (and not just prayers for marriage).
- Pastors and teaching elders: ensure that when the Word is ministered in your church, no one feels tacked on.

CHAPTER 4

> Marriage and families provide a rich source of potential problems to address, while I think singleness often is seen as only having the major problem of sexual temptation.
> ~ Katherine, Married

MIND THE GAP

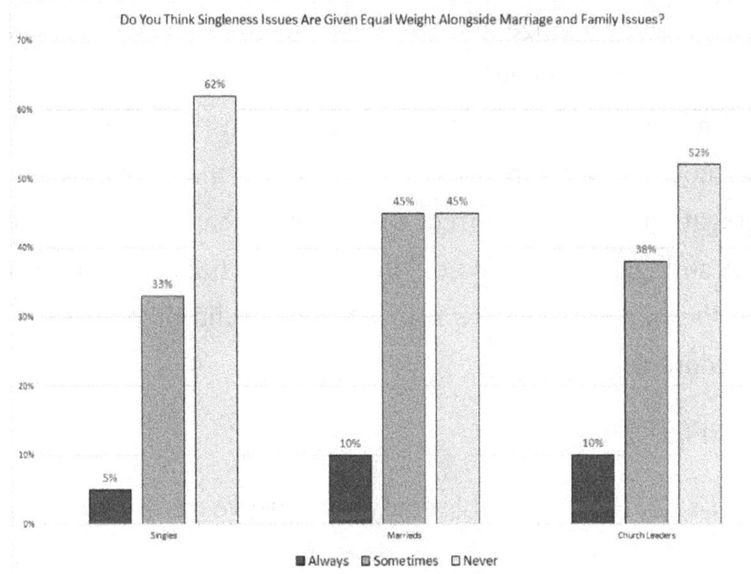

THE NUMBERS

Upon first blush, the statistics show some interesting symmetry. As you can see, marrieds and church leaders came to a general consensus regarding how much weight is generally given to singleness issues within the church. The comments, however, showed wide divergence of opinion regarding whether or not this situation is edifying or unedifying for a church body. While everyone seems to agree that marriage and family issues usually take precedence over singleness issues, not everyone agrees that the situation calls for change.

Just as pastors don't preach to fractured minorities, neither should congregations pander to them. Ministries, worship styles, church culture—all of it must be determined by the demographics of the church. Bending over backward to make each small cross-section feel as if it is the majority is counterproductive to unity. On this, we can probably all agree.

We must recognize, though, the difference between focusing too much on a marginal group and simply being aware of their needs and showing sensitivity to them. We must be careful that in trying not to overemphasize the needs of the singles in our congregations, we overcorrect to the point that we ignore their unique struggles. To do so could convey that because their needs are in the minority, they're somehow less valid or unworthy of being addressed.

THE DIFFERENCE

Let's say I attend a Bible study with twelve other women. It's a bad health week for the group. Five of us are currently suffering from head colds. We're coughing, sneezing, and hacking all over the place—admittedly a dismal experience. One woman in our group, however, suffers not from a head cold but from pancreatic cancer. Because she's in the minority when it comes to *type* of suffering, does that mean her need is somehow diminished by virtue of being less common? Of course not. Pancreatic cancer is serious. Despite our miserable head colds, the rest of us would take her condition seriously. We would pray for her, cook meals for her, drive her to chemo, and shave our heads together in solidarity.

However, just because cancer poses more danger than the

common cold, does that mean our friends with the colds don't have their own needs? Of course not. Anyone who's ever had a head cold knows how acute the suffering can be. We would also pray for those ladies, take them vats of soup, and volunteer to shoulder some of their afternoon activities so that they can nap in peace.

Although cancer is more serious than a head cold, when we all get together for our Bible study, we might actually spend more time talking about our colds than we do our friend's cancer. That doesn't mean we don't take her cancer seriously. It just means we have less to say about it than we do about our head colds. Because all of us have suffered from the common cold in the past, we understand this condition, empathize with how lousy it makes the sufferer feel, and can easily swap common cold horror stories.

THE GAP

I don't think any of the singles I interviewed believe that as members of a minority group within the congregation, they expect their needs to dominate church life. The question of equal weight is not one of equal *time*. Unfortunately, bridging the gap doesn't only mean talking about singleness stuff more often. While singles expressed frustration with feeling largely ignored, they also implied that they suspect their needs are seen as piddling problems—or not even as problems at all.

Allow me to illustrate with a personal example. I don't enjoy eating alone. As an extrovert, I believe good food and good conversation go hand-in-hand. It just makes sense to feed the stomach and the heart at the same time. What could be cozier?

But sometimes when I've expressed how lonely it is to eat meals by myself, my honesty has been met with sarcasm. In a misguided attempt to make me feel better while simultaneously highlighting their own struggles, some of my married friends have responded with some version of this: "You get to eat in peace and quiet without a toddler launching smashed peas at your head. Yes, I can see how that would be *very hard for you.*" My openness on these matters isn't always easy, and nothing makes me clam up more than this sort of emotional dissonance. In a moment ripe for empathy, such stonewalling makes me regret having opened up at all. Also, such responses can ignite feelings of guilt. Why am I struggling in the first place? Am I somehow out of line? I'm left wondering if everybody thinks there's something wrong with me for feeling lonely.

In such a situation, I'm not only concerned that my struggle with loneliness isn't being given equal weight. I'm concerned that it's not recognized as a legitimate problem.

WHY SINGLENESS ISSUES AREN'T GIVEN EQUAL WEIGHT

The Problems Are Unrecognized

As has been previously established, much of the gap in this area arises from the fact that singleness issues aren't always recognized as legitimate issues. This is the case for almost any outlying group: unless we've faced a particular struggle ourselves, we don't always recognize the seriousness. People don't intend to be thoughtless; they're just busy living their own lives and forget to look up, out, and around. They don't take time to know people well enough to empathize with their pain.

One of my hopes for this book is for readers to become more deliberate about getting to know the singles in their congregations through asking specific questions. Here are some good places to start:

- How can I pray for you this week?
- Do you want to have a coffee sometime? Go for a run? Take a walk? Go hunting upstate? Go to the beach? Come over and chat?
- What have you been studying in the Word? How has it helped you? Challenged you?
- Are you struggling with anything in particular lately?
- Are you looking for more fellowship/spiritual intimacy?
- Are you looking for an accountability partner?
- How do you feel overlooked at church? Why do you think that is?
- What do you wish we understood about your single life?
- How can I help?

It's worth mentioning that not every single will be open to this sort of dialogue. Unfortunately, some of the rudest, most inflexible people are singles who can't recognize that their self-centered independence must be balanced with deep community, full of complex and interconnected relationships. Such connections are difficult and messy. They require emotional commitment and self-sacrifice. However, until singles in this situation have their eyes opened by the Spirit, there's not a lot you will be able to do other than pray for them. (Not that prayer is a small matter.)

Problems Are Ignored

Most people feel ignored—single and married alike. As a general rule, we're all so consumed with looking after our own interests that we give little attention to the needs of others. This sin seems inherent in human nature, and even Christians are guilty. Apart from a specific spiritual gifting making us especially attuned to others, we tend to view our own issues as paramount.

That being said, statistics indicate that marrieds and church leaders feel they're already meeting the needs of singles; yet most singles don't feel that their needs are being met. Perhaps this is due to a disconnect between perceived needs and actual needs. Might singles feel ignored because they're looking for a different sort of support from what's being offered by their family, friends, and church families? Doubtless, there's room for better communication and growth on both sides, but the purpose of this book is to address what marrieds and church leaders can do to help.

To know how best to help the singles in your church, get to know them. Sit with them, eat with them, spend time with them. Once you've established a rapport, ask directly. It's hard to feel ignored when friends and leaders take an interest in your life, draw you in, allow you to exercise your specific spiritual gifts, and encourage you to grow. I speak from personal experience.

Now, you may find that when some singles confide in you, there may be some faulty expectations or self-centered thinking at the root of their struggles. If that's the case, correction is warranted. As brothers and sisters in Christ desiring to be conformed to His image, we have a responsibility to encourage and admonish one another in truth.[1] To that end, those who walk together must be open both to giving and receiving Scriptural correction.

True biblical correction rests in a spirit of meekness: we are not immune to temptation ourselves.[2] Likewise, approaching correction in a spirit of humility allows us to follow the biblical mandate to speak the truth in love.[3] Therefore, if you find you must correct a brother or sister, first spend time in prayer. Then proceed with grace and caution, understanding that encouragement, trust, a spirit of humility, and strong relationships help smooth the way.

Knowing whether or not correction is warranted, however, begins with establishing relationships. Since the needs of a single in any given congregation will be as diverse as each person, there's no point in giving advice here about what to do or how to help. Ask the questions, trust the guidance of the Spirit, and act accordingly.

Problems Are Misunderstood

Marrieds and church leaders often assume that if singles have unmet needs, they should solve their problems themselves. Not only will it give them something constructive to do with all of their free time, but it will also teach them a little about responsibility—which they're probably not learning any other way, given how frivolous and care-free the single life can be.

The messages seem to be that if singles are dissatisfied, at the very least they should speak up. Perhaps they should. Some of them, however, have already experienced having their expressions of need turned around on them or have experienced the conversation immediately turned into a lecture on how they need to learn to be content.

The problem with the "be content" talk is the underlying message it sends. It implies that if singles could simply learn to be content, they wouldn't *have* any more problems. At least, they wouldn't have any problems directly related to their singleness.

Not only is such advice not generally helpful, it's also not true.

In case I haven't mentioned this yet, at the time of this writing,

I'm thirty-nine years old, and I've never married. This wasn't my original life plan; but by God's grace, I've reached a level of contentment in my single life. It's not because I don't want to be married or because I've magically learned to "be content" with all of the difficult aspects of singleness. Mostly, I've learned to work with them and around them. It's helped that over the years, I've directly expressed my needs and have taken steps to meet the ones that can be met.

Take my discontent with lonely meal times as an example. Except for breakfasts (which were meant to be eaten alone, given the state of most human brains at that time of day), there are fourteen meals per week I might eat alone. Because eating alone makes me sad, I've taken some steps to whittle that number down. In other words, instead of gritting my teeth and learning to "be content" with solitary dining, I've worked together with family and friends to fill the gaps. Of those fourteen meals, I now eat four alone on average.

Herein lies the flaw in most of the contentment talks that I've heard over the years. In large part, the path to contentment doesn't come through some magical emotional shift (although God can certainly grant such shifts when they're necessary). Everything good in my life is a direct outflow of God's mercy and grace.[4] How could I not be content to rest in Who He is and what He's already given? He's saved and sanctified me through the ministry of the Spirit and the preaching of the Word. He's rooted me in a wonderful church family. He's surrounded me with a community of family and friends who regularly step up to meet one another's emotional and spiritual needs—mine included. To that end, I haven't hidden my needs from them.

This is why pastors, church leaders, and well-meaning

married friends must stop sending the message that the lone path to contentment for singles is through somehow passively learning to love the "single chapter" in their lives. Singles do not need to love everything about the "single chapter" to reach contentment. The issue is actually more complex. They must accept that singleness may be more than a chapter. It may be what God has planned for their whole lives.

When we view singleness as a "chapter," we tend to fall back on gritting our teeth and enduring. We settle for stop-gap measures instead of learning to live wholeheartedly in whatever situation we find ourselves. Remember, when Paul said he'd learned contentment in every situation, he wrote from a prison cell (Philippians 4:11); but he wasn't passively waiting for contentment. He was actively working toward what brought the greatest contentment: continuing to work for the Kingdom and shepherd souls through the means at hand.

In light of this understanding of contentment, singles must be allowed to be open about their struggles. Given how sensitive some singles are about these issues, striking the right balance here can be tricky. Some singles will assume slights, criticisms, and push-backs where none is intended. Unfortunately, we cannot do much about that. However, if openness from singles is only *ever* met with an admonition to suck it up and be content "for this season," their trust in you will waver and such transparency will dry up.

As Kelly M. Kapic writes in his book *Embodied Hope,* Christians must meld pastoral sensitivity with good theological instincts.

> Empathy and orthodoxy both matter. Benevolence and truth are meant to nourish one another, not to

> serve as two distinct options. When tenderheartedness and conviction are together, they bring life, but separated, they can be disastrous.[5]

As I read through the comment sections on the surveys, I found many singles commenting they had rarely been offered specific scriptural counsel regarding Christian singleness beyond the admonition to "be content." Simply admonishing a single to be content in the "single chapter" is like admonishing a struggling married couple to be content in their marriage without taking the time to get to the root of the issue. If a couple is struggling, we understand that there's an underlying reason that's probably not going to vanish on its own. The problems are doubtless complex and nuanced, and each couple needs to be addressed with compassion, understanding, and love.

> I understand that singles are in all stages of spiritual maturity, and have different interests, and may feel that their options are [either] be the Apostle Paul and have no personal or emotional needs or be a spiritual failure.
>
> ~ Sally, Married

The same is true of struggling singles. By coming to you, they've acknowledged their desire for individual counsel. Take the time to get to the root issues of discontentment before offering help, giving Scriptural counsel, or recommending practical steps. If needed, set struggling singles up with accountability partners and surround them with fellowship and love.

Marrieds must be sensitive to the individual needs of their single friends: building trust, asking questions, listening carefully, and reaching out in love to meet them if they can.

Singles should do the same for everyone else in the church.

The door hinges both ways, and we should all learn to cut each other some slack.

TO CHANGE OR NOT TO CHANGE

> Tell us when we married people are being hurtful in our words or actions. I like to believe that it is not intentional and that by being open, we can work toward something better.
> ~ Heather, Married

Ultimately, you must ask the Spirit for wisdom in analyzing how you approach singles. Not every church needs to make sweeping changes, and not every friendship needs to be completely reevaluated. According to the testimonies of singles surveyed, some of you are getting it right—in a big way. Some congregations, however, need improvement. If you've recognized the need for growth in this area, don't let this opportunity pass. A little change can make a big difference.

Discussion Questions:

1. Why is it sometimes counterproductive to tell singles to be content?
2. Am I close enough with my single friends to be aware of their daily struggles?
3. Am I ever guilty of trivializing someone else's needs because I can't see past my own situation?

Action Points:

- Ask singles about their daily struggles. Offer prayer and assistance as needed.
- Ensure that offers of counsel aren't always marriage and family oriented. Several survey takers commented that although their churches stress the importance of counseling for marrieds and soon-to-be-marrieds, the importance of counsel for singles seems overlooked. (Granted, these are subjective assessments; however, singles often mentioned feeling the need to chase down soul care. Why?)
- Let singles drive the conversation sometimes. Marriage and family issues can be overwhelming, but it's helpful and encouraging to hear about life from others' perspectives. Letting the singles drive the conversation will also ensure that they don't wind up feeling like glorified sounding boards.

> One of the biggest needs in the Christian fellowship arena is, I think, the need to see people as individuals rather than as a gender or as a marital status or as an age.
> ~ Katherine, Married

CHAPTER 5

SINGLES ONLY

When asked about the general effectiveness of singles ministry, the three survey groups had slightly different perspectives. This is not terribly surprising. A person's opinions regarding the effectiveness of singles ministries seemed strongly affected by whether or not he or she had participated in one. When those who *had not* participated in singles ministries were asked if they saw the value in such ministries, here's what they said:

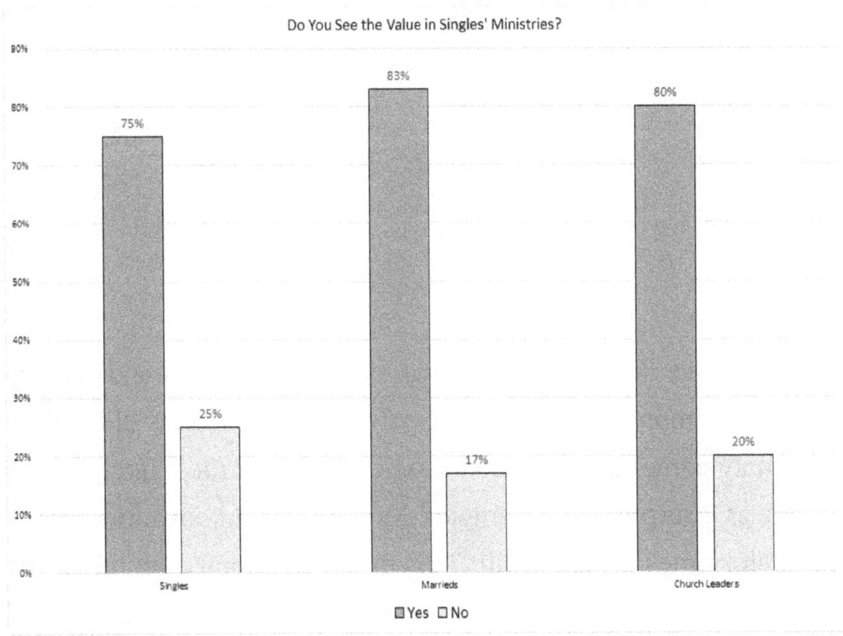

It's worth noting that the singles themselves seem to find the idea of singles ministry slightly less valuable than their counterparts. That's really not what I expected to see.

What's really fascinating, though, is what we see when we compare the numbers from those who *hadn't* participated in singles ministries with the data collected from those who *had.* When asked if their overall experiences with such ministries had been positive or negative, here's how the group who *had* participated in singles groups responded:

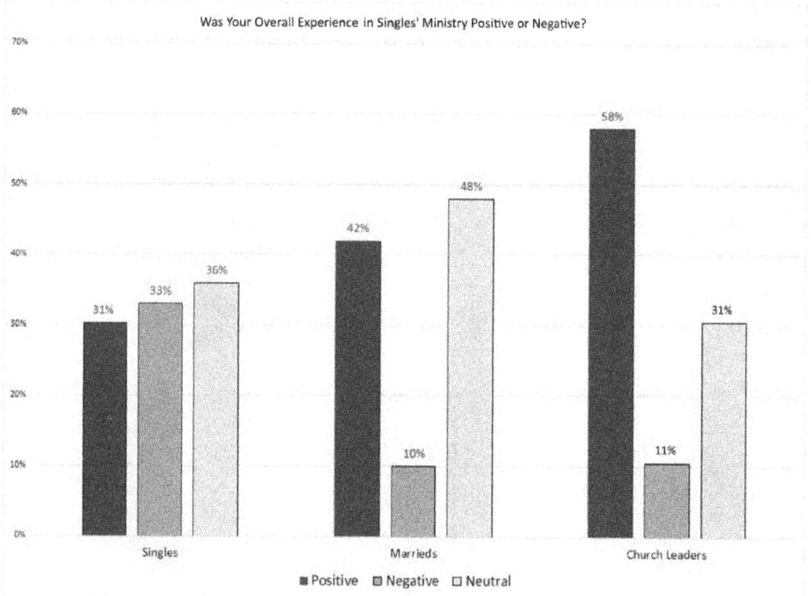

By and large, marrieds and church leaders found singles ministries more positive and effective than the singles did. While this may come as a surprise to some readers, it most likely won't come as a surprise to the singles. Most singles I know don't enjoy church singles groups at all. This may seem counterintuitive, but the reason might have something to do with the unspoken goal of most singles ministries.

> The singles ministry in churches can be a meat factory, and I am for certain every guy goes to find a girl, and most ladies go to find men. The singles group I used to be a part of had a lot of that going on, and I still see it to this day. The bad part about it is, when these relationships form and then break off it can cause dissention in the group. It takes away from the real meaning [of] why you are going in the first place, and can cause you to focus on the drama that was caused from the relationship(s).
> ~ Joe, Married

If the unspoken goal of many singles ministries is simply to allow unmarried members to mingle and connect, then it seems natural that the marrieds and church leaders would feel their time in singles ministry was successful. In fact, many married respondents said as much in their surveys: "Of course I see the value in such ministries! I found my husband/wife in one!"

Is this really all we ask for the effectiveness of our singles ministries? That they operate as a Christian dating service? That we herd the singles together so they can mingle, find one another, and hopefully, along the way, learn a few things that will prepare them for marriage? Marriage is certainly a calling worthy of great preparation, but so is all of life. What about preparing men and women for heartache, for spiritual warfare, for trials, for discouragement, for sexual

> I currently attend our church, but I skip out on the singles class. If I have to attend an hour of awkwardness on Sunday and an hour on Tuesday night I'm going to begrudge going to church.
> ~ Noah, Single

temptation, for grief, for failure, for *success* even? What about all of the singles who do not fit into the looking-to-marry category and find themselves ushered into a group whose primary function seems to be helping singles meet, match, and marry?

If you plan to justify your singles ministry as an actual ministry, then it must operate as more than a social club.

THE SHIFT

As early as 2012, the evangelical community recognized a definite trend away from singles ministries. In fact, *Christianity Today* announced that the church had entered "a post-singles ministry era."[1] Around the same time, a contributing writer for *Crosswalk* noted the particulars of the shift:

> Just as the number of singles is rising in churches across the country, churches across the country are axing peer-specific singles ministries. Only about 20% of North American congregations still have one, ranging in scope from the rare, full-blown worship services exclusively for singles, to more common weekly home groups, to monthly mixers.[2]

This trend doesn't necessarily mean the church has begun systematically abandoning ministry to singles. Far from it. In fact, there's evidence that this change actually improves genuine ministry. Instead of carving singles out of the congregation and relegating them to their own niche class operating more like a support-and-recovery group than anything else, many churches have opted toward a more inclusive model, one that fully integrates singles into the church family.

> If we are packaging the gospel for any specific demographic, we are failing in our call as the people of God. But if we are demanding that we be catered to as a specific demographic, we are exhibiting an equal error of selfishness. All around, we need to encourage a better ecclesiology of what it means to be the Body of Christ.
> ~ Richie, Married

Unless singles groups are given clearly-defined ministry goals, they can easily devolve into extended youth groups, keeping singles in a prolonged spiritual adolescence full of volleyball games and cookouts, its members skimming the surface of church life until they partner up and plunge into the full congregational experience. The same can be said of any group in the church that's routinely splintered off from the fold: youth groups, young adults, retirees, and so forth.

Of course, your singles ministry might be more than just a social club or a niche ministry catering to a specific demographic. It might provide genuine opportunities for spiritual growth, responsibility, and service. It might have real ecclesiastical value. If so, that's wonderful. You are to be commended.

If not, ask some stiff questions:

1) What is the function of this group—is it primarily social or spiritual?

2) Who leads this group—someone equipped with appropriate spiritual qualifications?

3) Why does this group exist—is there a Scriptural reason?

4) Does this group promote or enhance the spread of the Gospel, discipleship, and spiritual mentoring?

As I read survey responses, I came across the suggestion that singles be paired with mentors. I immediately became excited and felt like sending the respondent a virtual high five. Then I read the end of the comment: "Singles need mentors to prepare them and match them with someone suitable for them." Although finding a marriage partner could certainly be a positive byproduct of spiritual mentoring, it should by no means be its *end goal.* Because how short-sighted would that be?

Certainly, helping a Christian single to find a good spouse can be an aspect of ministry, but it seems a very personal ministry best suited to family and close friends (more on this later). For the church to have an entire arm of ministry solely dedicated to helping people pair off seems a bit silly. Unless you attend a megachurch, the singles in your congregations know each other. They should have no trouble finding one another socially without a special club designed to do this for them. If they can't, there's not really a lot a "singles ministry" will do to help them with that task, I'm afraid.

FRACTURED

In the spring of 2013, I fractured my ankle. Ironically, this happened while I was doing some agility exercises at the gym. (Oh, believe me. *I know.*) It was painful, embarrassing, debilitating, and frankly, a little ridiculous. As it turned out, my leg wasn't back in proper working order for nearly a year. That's the thing about fractures. They're always destructive, and without the grace of God, healing always takes longer than anticipated.

Americans live in an increasingly fractured society. Deprived of real community, most of us have lived without it so long that we barely register the loss. Further isolated through the cushions of wealth and privilege, we live as if we don't need each other in any real way: we rely on Google for information and advice, we pay a tow truck to pick us up when our cars break down, we let restaurants and food companies pre-prepare our meals, and the list could go on. Americans have turned being alone in a crowd into a lifestyle. Several factors contribute to this phenomenon.

> My take on "ministries" in church is that most of them wind up being social more than anything else. In that sense, I would like to fold singles into small groups that include young, old, families, singles, etc. [T]he small group would become a heterogeneous faith family—of which the single would be a part. I am not entirely convinced that a "singles group" would be healthy. The ones I have been familiar with seem to be a Christian lonely-hearts club full of needy people seeking fulfillment only in that Special Someone.
> ~ Nathan,
> Married/Church Leader

The first is that of mobility. According to data released by the U.S. Census Bureau in December of 2012, between the years of 2011 and 2012, 12% of the American population moved at least once—and that's considered a low figure by more recent standards.[3] I'd be the last person to say you should never move, but I do think the American tendency toward mobility often destroys our ability to build communities with deep roots. And why *are* we moving so much? To chase careers across the country? To seek the perfect neighborhoods, the perfect homes, and the perfect churches? At what expense?

Could it be that we cherish mobility at the expense of relationships?

The second factor contributing to our fractured society is one of national identity. America boasts a shared cultural narrative deeply steeped in the myth of self-reliance. Perhaps the typical American pictures himself as a modern-day Thoreau, ax in hand, striding purposefully into the woods on his way to live deliberately. (Until he remembers that despite being famous for writing a book about living in the woods alone, Thoreau didn't stay in the woods forever. Because … you know … *it was the woods*.) Although this sort of independent lifestyle sounds noble on the surface, it leads to some fairly disconnected lives. In fact, this aspect of American culture stands in opposition to much of the rest of the world, where extended families live more communally, supporting and loving each other in real, daily, tangible ways.

Could it be that we cherish autonomy at the expense of relationships?

Third, at least some of the fracturing of American society is intentional. By developing a disconnected set of differing peer groups—our gym friends, our church friends, our work friends, our book club friends, and our online friends—we can enjoy the simplicity of skimming from group to group, never really lonely, yet never experiencing true accountability. Such people can easily become a law unto themselves, navigating a series of distorted Venn diagrams with zero overlap. How are we to develop authenticity in our relationships if everyone we know is only allowed a sliver of our lives?

Could it be that we cherish individuality at the expense of relationships?

The church is depicted in Scripture as a Body: an interconnected whole. We're not a random jumble of body parts tossed together in a heap. We are bound—functioning together, not separately. That's why many congregations have moved away from the overly-programmed models of the 80s and 90s, in which members were pegged into specific ministry sections, only coming together (if at all) for one worship service a week. (Even then, the children were likely still in the Kid Zones.)

How can the older teach the younger if there's little opportunity for their lives to intersect? How can the strengths and weaknesses of singles and marrieds complement one another if the church draws a line of demarcation between singles and marrieds? How can the church incarnate Christ to the world if it's fractured? Its members must learn to live, love, and serve together in true multiethnic, multigenerational communities.

In his book *Life Together*, German theologian Dietrich Bonhoeffer speaks to the vital role Christian community plays in the life of the believer:

> [T]he Christian needs another Christian who speaks God's Word to him. He needs him again and again when he becomes uncertain and discouraged, for by himself he cannot help himself without belying the truth. He needs his brother man as a bearer and proclaimer of the divine word of salvation. He needs his brother solely because of Jesus Christ. The Christ in his own heart is weaker than the Christ in the word of his brother; his own heart is uncertain, his brother's is sure.[4]

I sincerely doubt the early church leaders segregated their services by generation, worship style, or marital status. We see no Scriptural evidence of such superimposed divisions. If they didn't do it, why should we?

ENTANGLEMENT

In order to better understand a concept, we usually step back to get the big picture. Instead, this time we're going to zoom in and examine something very small from the world of particle physics. (I know I promised not to scare you with any more math, but I said nothing about science.)

Quantum Mechanics is the study of the most basic elements of matter and the way they interact with one another. Within Quantum Mechanics is the process of Quantum Entanglement, a phenomenon that occurs at the most basic level of matter. Quantum Entanglement occurs when two particles physically interact with one another. Generally, two particles become connected because they originate in the same mass (although they can also be manually connected by researchers in a controlled environment). Once these particles have connected, they can continue to influence one other, even when separated by time and great distance.[5]

Due to Quantum Entanglement, two separate particles in two separate places can act in harmony with one another. Physicists have proven that if they measure the directional spin of one particle, they can determine the directional spin of the particle it's connected to. Because the particles are connected, their spins will always be inverse to one another.[6] Of course, I don't understand how this works—not *really*—but neither did the physicists who first floated the theory. Albert Einstein famously feuded with other physicists over this (and many other points). Einstein's understanding of physics was great, but—as we will discuss later—his own theories were largely influenced (and perhaps even hindered) by his own particular worldview.

Although my understanding of Quantum Mechanics may not be as great as Einstein's, I do know a bit about fostering connections on the human level—about what happens when we connect our lives and allow ourselves to be influenced by the people with whom we've connected.

Of course, this isn't as simple as it sounds. With all of the talk about how the world has become more interconnected through the power of advanced technology, there's no denying that society itself has become increasingly fractured. If Christians aren't careful, we could end up mirroring the trend rather than standing against it.

SPOOKY CONNECTIONS

When the theory of Quantum Entanglement was first advanced in the 1930s, Einstein didn't trust it. Specifically, he didn't trust the idea that particles could maintain their connection over such long distances. Their interactions over these distances would require communication faster than the speed of light, and that would conflict with his Special Theory of Relativity—a theory he'd built on a particular worldview. Because Einstein believed in an ordered universe—a universe in which "God does not play dice"—he was not comfortable with any theory which accounted the sort of randomness that the theory of Quantum Entanglement requires. He believed that what other physicists interpreted as randomness within Quantum Theory would one day be accounted for with some unknown, or "hidden" variable.[7]

Because of Einstein's discomfort with Quantum Entanglement, he dubbed the apparent connectivity of particles "spooky connections at a distance." Most likely, he used the word *spooky* merely to signify his unease with the premises of the scientific theory behind the phenomenon.[8] While I know it's not exactly what he meant, I can't help feeling that by using the word *spooky*, Einstein could be describing human connections as well as subatomic ones.

We could echo Einstein in calling human entanglements "spooky connections at a distance." First, any potential human connection existing between two members of a fallen race is "spooky": it's full of weakness, sharp edges, and sin. In a sense, all human beings are scary: they're selfish and needy and flawed. Maintaining deep, personal connections with even the nicest of them is fraught with peril. Second, any real human connection must survive separation over time and distance—if it doesn't, it probably wasn't much of a connection in the first place.

> I just feel like when a church has a ministry for every age group or special group of people, it does more to divide a body than unite it. I'm not saying a particular group of people doesn't have unique challenges. But if we only hang around people similar to us, we'll never be stretched to give in ways we wouldn't have thought, or carry one another's burdens in unique and different ways. We need everyone in the body to minister to each other. Not just the people we feel most comfortable with. Maybe this is one way a single can become more Christlike: insert themselves into a ministry that is totally out of their comfort zone.
> ~ Debby, Married

Weak relationships do not survive time and distance. Real ones do. Weak relationships do not guarantee influence. Real ones do. That's why we still find ourselves influenced by close friends who move across the country and why we're still influenced by our parents, grandparents, and mentors years after their deaths.

While downsides to personal entanglement certainly do exist, rich rewards remain. On this point, Scripture is clear.

Plans fail for lack of counsel, but in an abundance of counselors, there is safety. If two lie down together, they will keep warm, but how can one keep warm alone? A threefold cord is not quickly broken.[9]

I can see the value in gathering with people who have the same challenges and are in similar work/life patterns. I can also see the value in any Christians fellowshipping with other Christians, sometimes more value when people are more diverse, i.e. old with young, widowed with married, etc.
~ Marie, Married

I was part of a singles group that got together weekly to play volleyball and have a short Bible study afterward. It was a great support system and an enjoyable group. It wasn't affiliated with any particular church, and we took turns meeting in homes. Singles have different needs, difficulties, and goals than others, and it was nice to have that outlet. This was a vibrant, wonderful group.... Unfortunately, marriage destroyed the group in about five years.
~ Joanne, Married

Honestly, I don't think I would want a singles ministry. I would not like the awkwardness of "Oh, I'm single, I fit into this one category, and if and once I start dating I no longer fit there and have to leave, except if there's a break-up, I should go back to it." I would rather just be treated as a normal adult who just happens to be single, and for people to love me and care about me as such.
~ Anonymous, Single

There has to be a reason why God did not create human beings to be completely autonomous, self-propagating organisms. In His design, we all need one another. Just as He would not be complete if divided from the fullness of the Godhead, so we are not complete if we groundlessly divide ourselves from Him and from one another in the body of Christ.[10]

Within the world of particle physics, photons continue to influence each other's actions over great distances. In the greater world, we see a parallel truth. When we entangle our lives, we can't help but affect one another. Human hearts are profoundly shaped by the communities in which they allow themselves to become entangled; therefore, the rewards of true human connection, when done right, can greatly outweigh the spookiness.

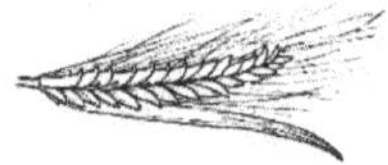

Discussion Questions:

1. How does the Scriptural teaching of Christians being members of one Body go against the grain of American self-reliance?
2. How do our church ministries foster connection or disconnection within the Body?

Action Points:

- Within church life, don't let singles isolate themselves. Do your best to integrate them into home groups with families.
- Include singles in group plans.
- Consider adopting a single into your family. Issue standing invitations for weekly meals and family game nights; become an emergency contact for singles living far from

blood relatives; involve them in discussions of holiday and travel plans. As bonds form and trust develops, encourage your children to think of these singles as members of the family.

CHAPTER 6

WHEN ENOUGH ISN'T ENOUGH

> I never really thought about being spiritually complete without being married. In theory, I suppose, yes, because Jesus is everything. But... even God said man did not need to be alone. I guess I don't have a true answer to that question beyond "I don't know."
> ~ Anna, Single

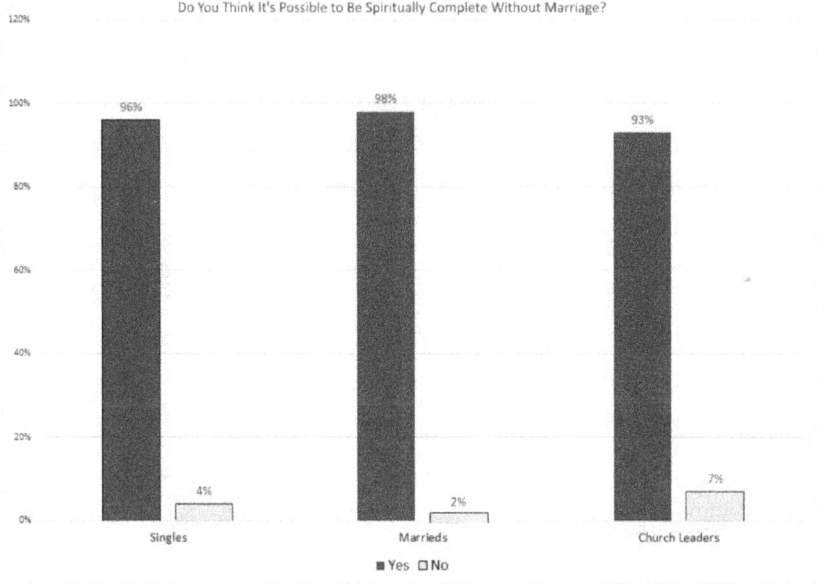

With a few exceptions, on this point, survey takers of all three groups agreed: although having a spouse can contribute greatly to developing Christlikeness through daily sacrifice and self-denial, marriage is not necessary for sanctification. What surprised me, however, was the 7% gap on the church leaders' side, especially since I expected the number to clock in at zero. Are there really so many church leaders who view singles as inherently spiritually deficient? If this attitude is coming from the pastors, no wonder so many singles feel dissatisfied with their church experience.

I followed up with the pastors to see if there was something else going on. You'll be happy to know that the 7% figure is due largely to a communication breakdown. In writing the survey, I should have offered a more complete definition of my terms. With this question, a simple clarification of the word *complete* would probably have greatly reduced the number of *no* answers.

As one pastor clarified, "I do not believe in Christian Perfectionism. During the sanctification process, it is impossible to be spiritually complete (whether married or single) due to the presence of sin. Completeness is a goal Christians aim for, but will not be realized until glorification." This pastor refers to sanctification's endgame: complete glorification through total union with Christ. That won't happen until we reach the eternal state. While we're still on earth, we undergo a steady process of being made holy through the Spirit of God applying truth to our lives.[1] That's called Progressive Sanctification, and it was the intended subject of my survey question.

The question, then, is whether married Christians have the edge on sanctification. Are spouses necessary to learn Christlikeness? Do marrieds have an advantage on the path to righteousness? Will singles stay forever trapped in spiritual immaturity?

DO YOU THINK IT'S EASIER OR HARDER TO BECOME CHRISTLIKE AS A SINGLE?

When I designed the survey, I left this question open-ended, meaning survey takers weren't given a set of answers from which to choose. Instead, they would need to articulate their own responses. Honestly, I'm not sure what I expected them to say. I knew what I thought the biblical response should be, but most of us have spent enough time in the church to know that perfectly nice church people can hold wacky ideas—some of them unbiblical. Frankly, that's not even a surprise anymore. Or so I thought. Despite approaching this section of the survey with low expectations, I still felt myself occasionally going a bit googly-

> I once had people in my church tell me I would never really understand how to pray and rely on God or have a deep relationship with Him until I had kids (I had been married for five years and hadn't gotten pregnant). I was very hurt and shocked at being judged as unspiritual ... Even though this happened years ago I have not forgotten how it felt to have a group of people—fellow church members—single me out like there was something wrong with me because my situation in life was different from theirs at the time. God taught me a lot about living for Him and not for other people's expectations, to be content and to be confident in His plans for my life. This incident has made me aware of a need for grace, kindness, and support among my brothers and sisters in Christ. It doesn't matter if they are single, married, childless, [or] a working mom: if they are where God has lead them then who am I to stand in their way? I should be supporting them and cheering them along their journey.
> ~ Anonymous, Married

eyed at the responses.

I was intrigued by the forceful minority of marrieds who insisted it must be harder to become Christlike as a single. Please know that I ask this question as gently as possible: How would you know? I'm genuinely curious because most who responded in this fashion offered almost no support for their opinions and seemed to be operating on flat conjecture.

Even more interesting were the individuals on both sides who assumed the *other* group somehow had the advantage. Marrieds said that it's probably easier for singles to devote time to study and service since they don't have the distractions of marriage and children. They pointed out that singles also theoretically have more discretionary income, meaning they're better suited to give sacrificially (since their sacrifices only involve themselves, not their children).

On the other hand, singles had their own assumptions regarding married life and Christlikeness. Some said marrieds have a better chance of becoming Christlike, pointing out that marriage provides daily opportunities to die to self through serving others and looking after needs other than their own, while singleness makes it all too easy to live for self.

> Perhaps what wearies me the most is the unending celebration and honor given to marriage and motherhood, as if it is the achievement of sainthood, the highest calling for any human. The highest calling for any life is to walk daily in God's purpose... I celebrate marriage, I honor motherhood... Motherhood is hard. Marriage is hard. And—shock of shocks—singleness is hard. We all need Jesus!
> ~ Anonymous, Single

In the end, neither of these theories proves wholly convincing. It's not marriage alone that truly fosters unselfishness, humility, and Christlikeness—it's the Holy Spirit working through the circumstance of marriage. It's not singleness alone that provides sufficient time for study, service, and sacrificial giving—it's the Holy Spirit working those circumstances for the good. Marriage and singleness both provide unique opportunities while simultaneously amplifying certain aspects of our sin nature which only the Holy Spirit can grind down to perfection.

Then why are these lopsided opinions so prevalent among believers? Why are we so quick to minimize the benefits of our own situations while concentrating on what we lack? Why is it so easy to make excuses and so hard to get it right?

INSIDE OUT

We'd all like to think other people have the inside track and that what holds us back from achievement is our particular situation. I think it's human nature to assume that when we have a hard time, it must be because we lack an edge others enjoy and that the only thing holding us back is the one thing over which we have no control. (Not that we have no control over whether or not we're married or single, but the point stands.) It's easy to ponder how much more spiritual we would be if our situations were different. It's hard to address our current issues directly. When we view other people's situation from inside our own experience, not only are we in danger of making false assumptions about *them*, but we also risk failing to see ourselves clearly.

> While I answered that I do believe I can be complete in Christ and be single, I have had it implied from my married friends that I could not understand true sanctification until I am married...maybe I don't know because I'm not married, but I believe that may be a sadly short-sighted view of the Holy Spirit's work.
> ~ Anonymous, Single

The survey responses also reveal some deeper assumptions at

work. More than just revealing the subconscious excuses we make for our own lack of spiritual development, these answers strike at the very core of what it means to be Christlike. Are we Christlike because we serve or because we learn? Are we Christlike because we're growing or because we're giving?

The answers, of course, are *yes* and *yes*.

What It Really Means to Be Christlike

To be Christlike means we reflect the image of God fully. Jesus Christ was (and still is) the only "real" man who's ever walked the earth—perfect, sinless, and fully surrendered to the will of the Father. While Adam and Eve displayed uncorrupted human nature in their innocence, Christ displayed a perfection that underwent temptation and trial.

While fully God during his time on earth, Jesus was still fully man, exposed to all of the weakness inherent to the human condition. Says Dorothy L. Sayers,

> …that for whatever reason, God chose to make man as he is—limited and suffering and subject to sorrows and death—he [God] had the honesty and the courage to take his own medicine ... He has himself gone through the whole of human experience, from the trivial irritations of family life and the cramping restrictions of hard work and lack of money to the worst horrors of pain and humiliation, defeat, despair, and death. When he was a man, he played the man. He was born in poverty and died in disgrace and thought it well worthwhile.[2]

While Sayers may not have fully understood why Christ had to come as a man, other theologians are mindful that since sin occurred in and through a human body, it must be overcome in and through a body.[3]

As a result of the redeeming work of Christ, the effects of the fall on our eternal destinies are reversed. Though once hostile to God through our sin, we now reconciled to Him and are being conformed to His image—He who is the image of the invisible God (Colossians 1:15). As the Holy Spirit uses the Word of God to make us increasingly aware of our sin and our ongoing need to repent and change, we increasingly reflect His image. Meditating on the fullness of Christ's earthly life can help us fully understand our original question about Christlikeness.

Jesus wasn't a perfect expression of the Godhead because he *just served* or *just sacrificed* or *just taught*. Jesus didn't *just* anything. He expressed the complete union of perfected humanity. Full divinity, wrapped in humility. That's the Holy Spirit's target for each of us. Not that we will become gods ourselves, but by allowing the Holy Spirit to sanctify us from the inside out, we reflect Christ to the world. We're all called to this: singles and marrieds alike. Both the single state and the married state present unique opportunities to allow Christ to shine through us.[4]

A friend once said that one of the reasons there are so many different personality types could be that it takes many "images" to reveal even a fraction of Who God is. By allowing Him to amplify our strengths and eliminate our weaknesses, together the Church can create a dazzling kaleidoscope of the true image of God through which His light can radiate outward to the world in beauty and power. This will only happen if we're willing to let Him smooth our sharp edges, sand us down, re-shape us, frame us, and fit us together like so many puzzle pieces. We must bear in mind, however, that our conformity is not a ritualistic obedience intended to gain His favor but the result of overwhelming gratitude for the grace He's already bestowed.

It's not an easy process, nor a pretty one. In Romans 7:18-20, Paul eloquently expressed his angst over the process of moving from sinner to saint:

> "For I have the desire to do what is right, but not the ability to carry it out. For I do not do the good I want, but the evil I do not want is what I keep on doing. Now if I do what I do not want, it is no longer I who do it, but sin that dwells within me."

Who among us wouldn't echo some version of this struggle? Whatever our current situation when it comes to relationships, we're all going to wrestle with the process of conforming to the image of Christ. The battle will be easy for exactly none of us.

> I think that people who are single become Christlike in different ways than people who are married. From what I hear, people who are married often become more Christlike in areas of sacrifice and compromise. I think people who are single often become more Christlike in areas of dependence on Christ and living in a community broader than a marriage.
>
> ~ Anonymous, Single

The Struggle is Real

Christlikeness is the ultimate struggle, and the struggle is real. I don't care who you are—single, dating, engaged, thrice-married or life-long celibate. Nobody gets a fast-pass to perfection. We're all in this together—you, me, and every other believer in the world. The question is not how much easier Christlikeness would be if we found ourselves in a different life situation. Such thinking smacks of self-justification and excuses. The question is what to do now to ensure that we don't use our current situation as a cop-out.

Each circumstance comes with separate benefits and afflictions. Instead of tallying our scoresheets and focusing on what's wanting, we must focus instead on maximizing the benefits and asking the Spirit to help us develop in the areas of weakness.

> I sometimes wonder why married people don't make a point to be encouraging. Why can't they ever say, 'I really respect your love for the Lord and am cheering for you to be pure and faithful to truth your whole life'?
> ~ Anonymous, Single
>
> 
>
> In some cases, I think it could be incredibly beneficial to have another person encouraging you to become more like Christ and to help keep you accountable. On the other hand, isn't that what discipleship is? And aren't we commanded to do that anyway, with or without a spouse?
> ~ Sarah, Single

Singleness is not the path to committed study and church service any more than marriage is an automatic graduate course in selfless living. Although each situation may lend itself more naturally to those lessons, that doesn't mean that A) the individuals in those situations will take full advantage of growth opportunities, or that B) said situations are the only possible way to develop those traits. In Scripture, the most valuable lessons are not taught through ease. Deep truths are generally revealed through furnaces, crosses, and storms. The gate to salvation is narrow, its path stippled with blood drops and littered with thorns. And we are called to follow those steps.

Therefore, instead of bemoaning their lack of accountability, singles should actively seek ways to build more of it into their lives. Likewise, marrieds can strive to appropriate their time wisely, making study and service a priority, even if it involves losing sleep. Professional athletes don't use their weaknesses as excuses for not bringing home the gold. They adjust their training to address those weaknesses *in order* to bring home gold. May we learn to do the same.

> Not that I have already obtained this or am already perfect, but I press on to make it my own, because Christ Jesus has made me his own. Brothers, I do not consider that I have made it my own. But one thing I do: forgetting what lies behind and straining forward to what lies ahead, I press on toward the goal for the prize of the upward call of God in Christ Jesus. Let those of us who are mature think this way, and if in anything you think otherwise, God will reveal that also to you. (Philippians 3:12-15)

Discussion Questions:

1. What makes a person truly Christlike?
2. In what ways have I used my situation to subconsciously excuse myself for not having developed in certain areas of Christlikeness?

Action Points:

- Call to check in with a single this week.
- Extend offers of spiritual accountability to singles. Do not judge or shame them when they come to you for help, confession, spiritual encouragement, or support.
- In all matters, point singles to Christ.

> My biggest issue with the church and single people is this thinking that single people are not fulfilling God's purpose.
> ~ Courtney, Single

CHAPTER 7

PERCEPTIONS AND MISCONCEPTIONS

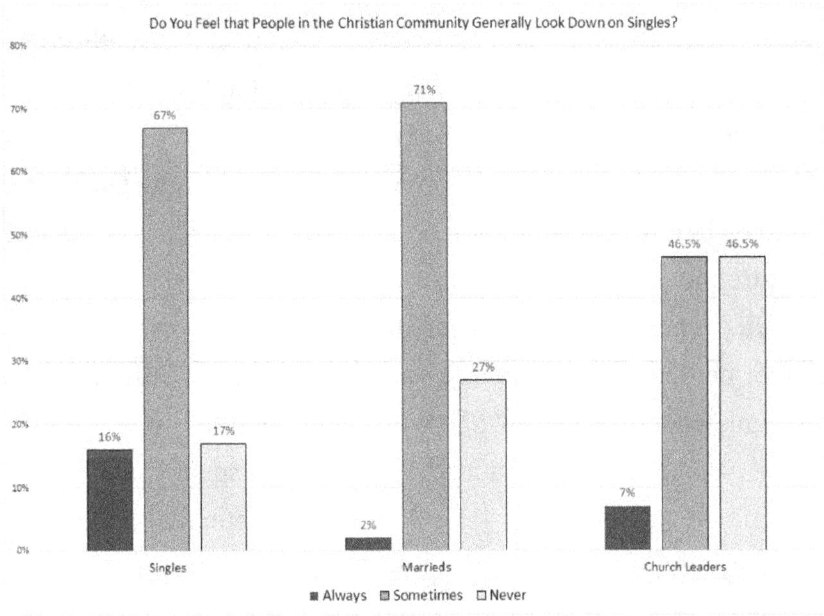

We'd all like to think it's uncommon for singles to feel looked down on by their fellow church members. Occurrences in my own experience have been fairly rare, with such cases almost always taking place outside the comfort of my own home church. Sadly, the numbers reported from singles tell a different story. Not only do 67% of the singles surveyed admit to feeling looked down on for their singleness *sometimes,* but 16% of singles surveyed also feel that the Church *always* looks down on them. If you add those two categories together, it means a total of 83% of church-going singles have felt looked down on in church to some degree. While marrieds and church leaders aren't completely tone-deaf to this perception, the statistics aren't particularly encouraging.

Is this 83% a statistic that any of us can feel comfortable with? Why is the percentage so high? Do that many people in the church look down on singles for not being married? Are the singles just overly sensitive? Is there something else going on here? Perhaps.

Based on my own experiences, the problem seems to be mostly generational. The most insensitive comments usually come from individuals in my parents' age bracket (the Boomers). These men and women (but mostly men) are the ones responsible for the lion's share of the pointed comments and awkward, guffawing jokes. They're also commonly the ones grilling us about our catastrophic love lives in front of a spontaneous *ad hoc* jury of our church peers. To be fair, these are the same people who often make dumb, depressing statements about marriage, too: "Just wait 'till the honeymoon's over!"; "She won't look like *that* in ten years"; "Now you're stuck with him!" It's hard to square this sort of discourse with Ephesians 4:29: "Let no corrupting talk come out of your mouths, but only such as is good for building up, as fits the occasion, that it may give grace to those who hear."

In addition to less-than-kind comments and un-funny jokes, other forces may shape the singles' perception that they're looked down on at church. To clarify: I really don't think many churchgoing people actively look down on or think less of singles for being unmarried, but I do think the 83% figure is a direct result of church members accidentally having given the impression that they do.

HOW TO IMPLY THAT YOU LOOK DOWN ON SINGLES (ACCIDENTALLY)

Ask a Single "What's Wrong with All These Guys/Girls?"

When you say this, you probably mean to imply that the single in question is not to be faulted for being single; however, what the single often hears is that there's a fault in being single—a fault serious enough to require placing blame.

Also, as comments go, it's frustratingly unanswerable.

1) If we say "Nothing's wrong with all these guys/girls," then we're tacitly admitting that there must be something wrong with us, since as the scenario is presented, someone must be at fault.

2) If we start ticking off a list of what's actually wrong with all these guys/girls, then we come across as critical and exacting, perhaps confirming the suspicion that we're still single because we're just too choosy.

May I humbly suggest that this comment be jettisoned completely? Instead, say what is actually meant: "I think you're an incredible, talented person; I recognize your value." To speak such a comforting and affirming word directly is greatly heartening; however, to hinge a compliment on marriage, (i.e., "I don't understand why a nice guy like you still isn't married,") can inadvertently imply that marriage is the crowning achievement of valuable people and that someone's worth somehow isn't validated unless he's married.

Readers who recall having said a version of this phrase to a single friend shouldn't beat themselves up, however. On one level, most singles understand where you're coming from. On the other hand, it's hard to explain how these comments sound after repeated cycles—especially to singles who long for marriage and might already doubt their own worth as a result. Don't add fuel to the fire. It tends to burn brightly enough without outside help.

TELL SINGLES THEY WILL UNDERSTAND BETTER WHEN THEY'RE MARRIED

Unless the topic they'll understand better when they're married is What It Feels Like to Be Married, saying singles will understand any given topic better once they're married implies a belief that singles are spiritually, emotionally, or intellectually stunted and will remain so unless they wed. This view is false.

We don't need to experience all aspects of life in order to speak to them—otherwise, how would pastors pastor, counselors counsel, and parents raise children with talents, interests, and life experiences different from their own? Although we may lack true empathy without a shared personal experience, we can still offer sympathy, wisdom, knowledge, or a valuable alternate perspective. An oncologist need not experience cancer himself to understand the disease and advise treatment. In the same way, adults need not be married to understand the various trials of life. Marriage is certainly the vehicle God uses to drive specific truths home, but that does not mean He must use the same vehicle for everyone. That's why Paul and Jesus gave plenty of advice without being married—they gave advice about *marriage,* even. Marriage is not a requirement for spiritual sensitivity,

> Unfortunately, I feel like the church has put singles in a separate "class." I definitely don't think that it's intentional, but people make you feel like your opinions/efforts aren't valid unless you are married.
> ~ Anonymous, Single

intellectual clarity, or relational understanding. Implying the opposite casts doubt on the facility of the Holy Spirit, who has been sent to teach us "all things" regardless of whether we're single or married, male or female, bond or free (John 14:26).

Imply that Marriage and Family Are Inevitable

Growing up hearing "when you get married" and "when you are a husband/wife someday" can take its toll on the psyche, especially if the years roll by and no marriage reaches fruition. Contrary to popular Christian folklore, marriage is not an inalienable right promised by God as a reward to the faithful, and we shouldn't imply that it is. If we do, we undermine more than just the Bible's teaching on marriage.

My generation of Christian Singles grew up on a wave of *I Kissed Dating Goodbye*[1] culture, in which we were taught that if we didn't date recreationally and if we kept ourselves "pure" by not having sex before we were married, God would reward us with dreamy Christian spouses who had also saved themselves for us. We would all have wonderful relationships with sex lives worth the wait.

Of course, much of that idea is problematic—not that the Christian community seemed to recognize the fly in the theological ointment at the time. It was an era of purity pledges, purity rings, and purity balls.

Purity is about much more than just not having sex (as Jesus clarified in Matthew 5, and we will discuss further in Chapter 13), and encouraging young adults to keep their bodies pure for a future spouse is short-sighted, if not idolatrous. We do not stop with keeping our bodies sexually pure for a future spouse. The issue runs deeper than that. We strive to keep our entire selves pure for

Christ—body, mind, heart, and soul. He is our true Spouse and ultimate heart's desire. Marriage is a shadow: He is the reality.

Teaching men and women to keep themselves pure for reasons other than the glory and pleasure of their Maker is a matter for concern. Purity for the sake of others is biblical (as in abstaining from doubtful things so as not to cause others to stumble), but if we seek purity for our own ends in order to gain something from God, we practice idolatry.

To pledge purity for self-interested reasons is also potentially embittering. If the marriage doesn't work out or the sexual union is not wholly satisfying, Christians might feel they have the grounds to turn to God and say, "I saved myself for *this?* I thought we had a deal!"

In his book *The Prodigal God,* Timothy Keller identifies this sort of give-and-take attitude with the elder brother in the parable commonly known as "The Prodigal Son." The elder brother became resentful over his father's grace toward the younger son because he felt that through his long obedience (his "purity"), he had earned certain rights—specifically, a right to the family's wealth. Says Keller, "In this same way, religious people commonly live very moral lives, but their goal is to get leverage over God, to control Him, to put Him in a position where they think He owes them."[2] This is not the sort of twisted theology we want to encourage among our Christian brothers and sisters, even inadvertently. We do not love, obey, honor, serve, or cherish God in order to get anything from Him—other than Himself.

As I stated earlier, I don't think the majority of Christians actively look down on singles. Could it be that the minority who do are responsible for causing 83% of singles feel looked down on? Maybe.

> I think it would be useful for pastors and other church leaders to remember that everyone is single at some point in life. We all start out single. Many of us will be widowed or divorced. The Christian family does not consist of Mom, Dad, and the 2.5 kids.
> ~ Nancy, Single

But what are we to make of the 16% who *always* feel looked down on?

Yes—it could be that some of the singles are oversensitive and perceive slights where none are intended. We've all known such people. It could also be that the 16% who always feel judged attend churches in which the leadership talks down to/about singleness from the pulpit, causing this attitude to permeate the entire ministry. Pastors may fail to take singles' unique situations into account when preparing sermons, falling back on the sort of tacked-on comments previously discussed. It bears mentioning again at this point because it sends the subtle message that singles are somehow second-class citizens and could contribute to why singles are feeling looked down on.

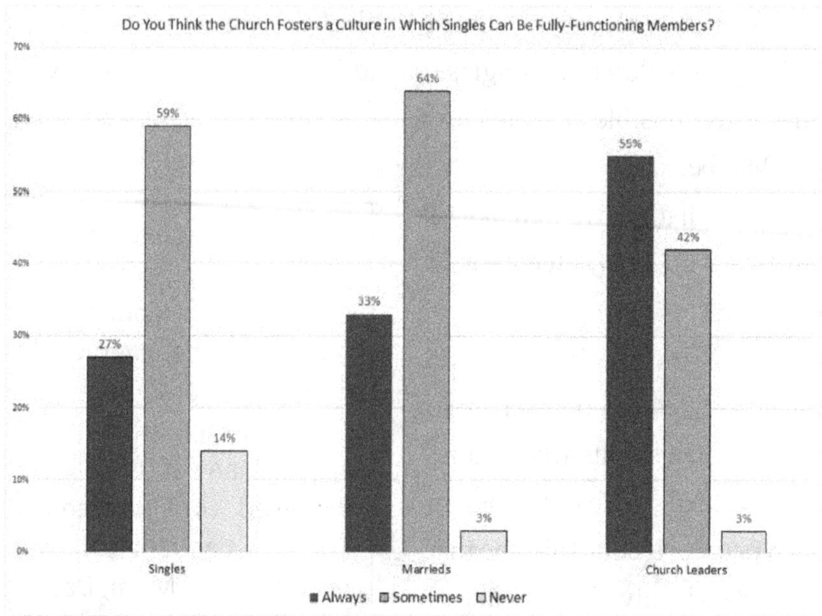

I'M AN OUTLIER

It's discouraging to see that only 27% of singles believe the Church always allows them to be fully-functioning members. As I read through the survey responses from other singles, I realized how much of an outlier I am. Although I've never been married, I've held a wide variety of leadership positions in my church over the years. I've never felt that any of my acceptance or worth in the church hinged on my marital status. Leadership has trusted me to head committees, lead trips, teach classes, and practice my spiritual gifts. While I'd like to credit my church for just being really good at handling the whole singles-and-service issue, there's another factor in play. Because I still attend the church in which I grew up, and because I've been faithful there for many years, the fellow members know me inside out. They trust me. I'm not typecast as a rootless free spirit or loose cannon. They've seen my spiritual gifts develop over time and know the amount of education

I've received. Because I've been in the church from my youth, I've been going through the vetting process my entire life.

I sometimes wonder, however, what my experience as an unmarried woman would be if I were to move. Would my Hypothetical New Church be as eager to use me in the specific areas of my giftedness? I have no way of knowing unless I were to try. The feedback I received from other singles in the survey doesn't make the prospect seem attractive.

If we adopt the mindset that the end goal of adulthood is marriage, or that marriage is a reward for good behavior and the only assured path to spiritual development, then we will reserve roles of leadership, teaching, and influence for married members only. As it stands, most churches seem fine with having the singles chip in with their share of church work (because look at how much time they have to serve!); however, we should not confuse being "active" in the church with feeling fully integrated. We must allow singles to serve in the specific areas of their giftedness. We must include singles on boards and committees, ask them to teach, and consider them for leadership roles when appropriate. To fail to do so is a huge disservice, both to the singles and to the Church.

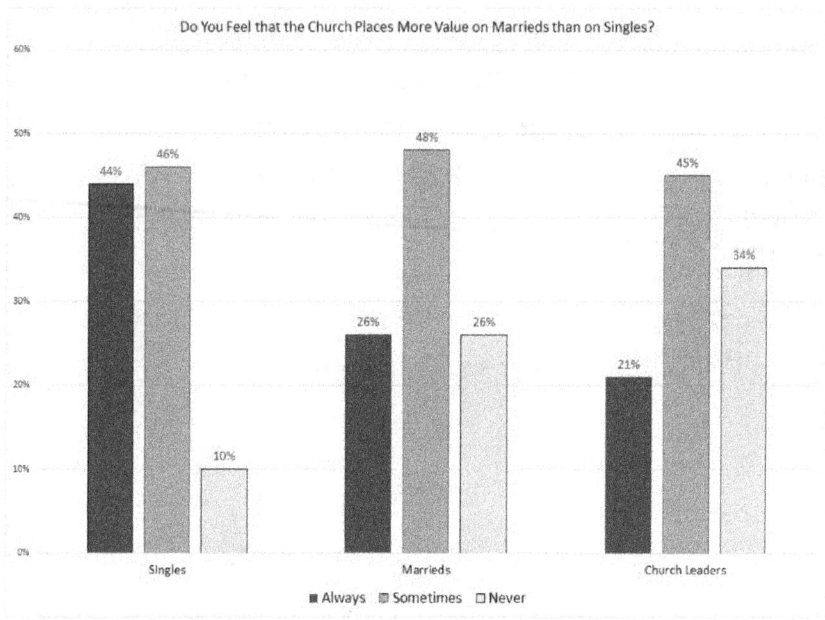

While the church leaders usually maintain a consistent divergence from the other two groups, this time it's the singles who diverge. As you can see, singles are fairly well split in their responses, with only 10% responding that marrieds are *Never* considered more valuable in the church, leaving the rest to divide themselves nearly evenly between *Always* and *Sometimes.* Based on the comments made in the survey, singles feel very strongly about this issue; therefore, the fact that neither the majority of the marrieds nor the church leaders seem in step with the singles' perceptions raises serious concerns.

COMMENTS SINGLES MADE ABOUT FEELING UNDERVALUED

- [The Church] places a lot of value on families and people with children. Not a lot of what a single person does is celebrated like what married people do.

- I don't know if *value* is the right word. I just think the Church doesn't know what to do with [singles], because it's so contrary to what society has always been, especially as singles get older.
- [It's] all about Focus on the Family. Marriage is seen as the solution to fornication, homosexuality, liberalism, etc., and if you're single, people think you might be susceptible to one of those.
- They see couples as a greater asset to ministry. Singles are looked at more as lone rangers.
- I think the message is often, "If you are married, you are complete. You have arrived."
- Married people have realized their potential [for] adding people to the family of God. Single people haven't made it yet.
- I think most churches (like my church) want to grow, and they think that the key to growth is young families.
- I think that in the church, singles are viewed [as] not-really-developed Christians. So, they're not often asked to lead.
- [Sometimes the Church] seems to make it easier for married couples to get involved.

REASONS SINGLES MIGHT FEEL UNUSED AND UNDERVALUED

They're Not Seen as Settled

As one survey respondent already pointed out, often singles are stereotyped as Lone Rangers. Although some of them certainly *might* be, there's no reason to consider people less grounded simply because they're unmarried.

Case in point: I held my last job for twelve years and my current job for five. I've only moved twice within the past decade, both local moves due to changing housemate situations. I've attended the same church for almost my entire life; and while I do enjoy traveling, I only take one "big" trip a year—a trip generally lasting fewer than two weeks. On weekends, I keep nearly the same schedule I do during the week, going to bed early and getting up early. Yet I've still been asked when I'm going to "settle down."

What is meant, of course, is when do I plan to marry; however, American society has so equated marriage with "settling down" that some assume anyone not married must therefore not be settled. If this bias seeps into the church, it can needlessly disqualify singles from positions in which they could best exercise their spiritual gifts.

All Leadership Qualifications Are Standardized to the Highest Level

In the New Testament, God gave very clear instructions to the Church regarding the qualifications of pastors, deacons, and elders. With these, I have no quarrel; however, problems arise when local churches seek to make the biblical qualifications for those three offices the qualifications for *all* leadership positions. (These may be the same types of churches which require full-fledged membership before they'll allow someone to pass out a bulletin.)

I'm not saying you should throw away standards for leadership. I am saying you should carefully consider *why* you hold those standards. If your standards are fully biblical, hang on for dear life. If they're not, reevaluate.

HOW TO REEVALUATE

Pray

As with any other aspect of your ministry, start by making this issue a matter for prayer. Ask the Holy Spirit to open your eyes to what (if anything) should be adjusted.

Poll

Conduct a straw poll among your church's singles to see what their experiences have been in these matters. You may choose to ask these questions in person or in small groups. In that case, plan to listen without offering immediate defense or argument. If you think singles might be freer with their answers via a more indirect medium, plug these questions into your church website and give the option for an anonymous response.

Assess

Not only should you weigh the data from your straw poll, but you should also assess the methods your church uses to select leaders. Every church, no matter how effective, has blind spots. Survey results reveal that more than a few churches have room to grow.

> Singles do have value in the church and community even though a lot of people seem to [overlook them]. There are those of us that hear you!
> ~ Rachel, Married

Plan

After you've prayed, polled, and assessed, use what you've learned to make a plan. With just a few minor adjustments (mental adjustments more than anything else), most churches can effect changes that will leave their singles feeling more valued and fully-integrated than ever before.

Discussion Questions:

1. What are the biblical mandates relating to marriage and holding church offices?
2. Does our church make teaching and leadership roles open to qualified singles? Why or why not?

Action Points:

- Check your church's leadership requirements for possible unbiblical bias.
- Connect your singles to ministries that allow them to practice their unique spiritual gifts.

CHAPTER 8

WHEN HARRY MET SALLY (AND THE WHOLE CHURCH GOT INVOLVED)

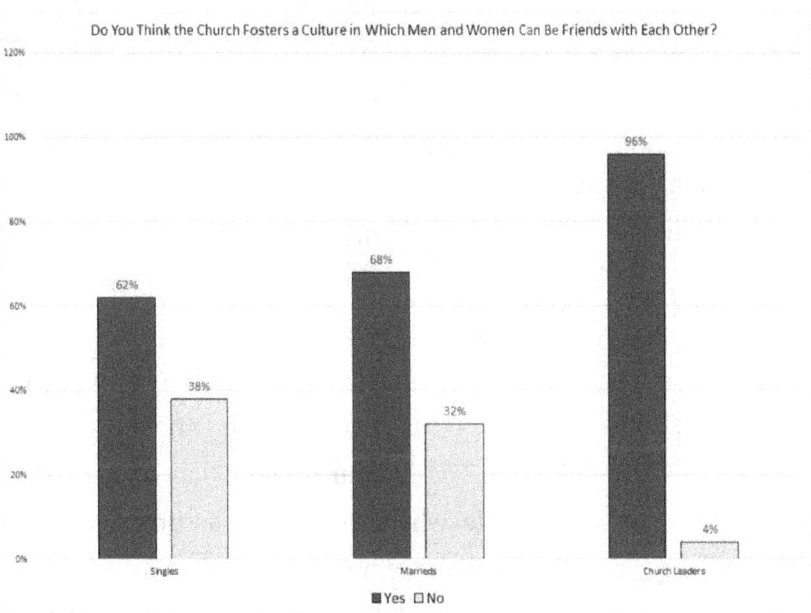

I know a man and a woman who are friends. They've known each other for a long time, and although they're separated by distance, they keep in touch. These two are not particularly attracted to each other—they both know that. They've discussed their relationship, and it's not that either has put the other in the Friend Zone. They've always been friends, with no desire on either side for anything else. Yet it feels sometimes that they're secret friends. Why? Because they're two of the lone single hold-outs from their college peer group, and they've both been pressured by mutual friends to date each other. They're both tired of riding the explanation merry-go-round that starts up when married friends spot them interacting. It's just easier to keep their friendship on the down-low.

Keeping a friendship "on the down low" sounds sort of shady. It's not shady at all, but it's easy to imagine how some married friends or church leaders might react to hearing this story. Before jumping to any conclusions, however, know that many singles taking my survey have experienced similar frustrations. In fact, on reading an early draft of this chapter, one single (a thirty-two-year-old never-married) immediately launched into a story about how the people where she works assumed she was dating a young man because the two were great friends, got along well, and displayed real affection for each other—affection built through having grown up together in church. The idea that

> My church is totally fine; but I've been in churches where they are utterly paranoid and think that any male-female interaction will eventually lead to something illicit, so they make a supreme effort to keep proper (often artificial) boundaries. And yet they are, paradoxically, trying to get couples married at the same time.
>
> ~ Anonymous, Single

> Most people assume that if a man and woman are friends, then something else is either happening or is due to happen. It's not really specific to the church. That said, a lot of church people seem very, very cautious about male/female friendship if one or both of them happen to be married.
>
> ~ Jessica, Single

affection can exist without romance is boggling to those outside the faith. Should the same be said of those inside the church?

FRIENDSHIP FRUSTRATIONS OF SINGLES

When filling out their surveys, singles expressed a wide variety of friendship frustrations. Below is just a sampling.

- I feel that single men and women are placed in an awkward position in the church. They usually are expected to couple up.
- I don't seek close friendships with men because they seem to lead to the men thinking that we are headed for a relationship.
- People tell me to avoid friendships with the opposite gender because I'm only playing with fire.
- The church doesn't foster a culture in which men and women can be friends. I don't know if this is the fault of the church or the reflections of societal values [influencing] the church.
- I think there is suspicion of single people, especially single women when it comes to opposite-sex friendships. Overall, I think that men and women are separated out from each other except when acting as couples.
- If I have some geeky shared interest with a guy at a church, I can't really build a friendship off of that because someone will bring up the whole "avoid the appearance of sin" thing. No, we're talking about Doctor Who, not running off to Mexico together.
- It really feels like the implication is that I can totally ruin a marriage by trying to make friends.

- I believe a man and woman can be close friends with no intimate involvement, but the church makes that awkward or assumes there has to be more.
- Women tend to talk about topics related to their roles as wives and mothers. Because I'm neither of those things, I find that I have more in common to talk about with the men. I don't want to earn a reputation as a woman who's out to get attention from the guys, though, so I just sit through lots of discussions that I don't take part in.
- There is a single man in our church. We became friendly and started doing things together. Up front, we both established boundaries: [friends], nothing more. So we are going out to movies, plays, dinner at least two times a week… *Immediately*, everyone in church wants to know if we are steady… They all wanted us to get married [because] that is the goal: to get a husband. We felt so much pressure. I enjoyed the friendship; I felt safe; no pressure from him to pursue a relationship. And now I deal with church friends who are happy that we are no longer friends and others who are now praying for me to find "another man."
- They preach no premarital sex, so I don't see why they would feel people couldn't be friends, but they warn against spending alone time with the opposite sex, so I'm not sure. Also, it feels like they preach that women are a temptation, so they should be avoided if you feel attracted to them.
- [It's] not that the church discourages friendships. The problem is that every friendship comes under suspicion of potential romance, which can blow the opportunity to [be friends].

- I feel there is a weird stigma around single women and married men in the church. Like my status as an unmarried woman automatically makes me a temptress that wives have to watch their husbands around. No one will say that aloud, of course, but there is a definite aura of disapproval if a single woman is friends with a married man, rather than being friends with his wife.
- I'd like to be more open and friendly with single men who visit my church—on a friendship basis—but I end up avoiding them because of everyone's close scrutiny and assumptions and questions. It's just a hassle.
- I think purity culture has a lot to do with male/female friendships being problematic. If we didn't go around assuming that every male is inherently lecherous and every woman is inherently seductive, friendships (and even potential relationships) could grow a lot more naturally.

WHY SINGLES ARE HYPER-SENSITIVE

Perhaps singles are overly sensitive about friendship because they feel that without a spouse, they not only lack deep intimacy with the opposite sex, but they also miss the chance for the sort of built-in, cross-gender friendship that can develop when couples bond with other couples. While it's not fair to assume that all married people enjoy these benefits, it's easy to see why singles feel that they're missing out. Many struggle to build appropriate cross-gender friendships within a recognizable Christian-culture framework.

When singles do develop friendships with the opposite sex, however, the pressure for the friendship to develop into "something more" instantly begins. In some cases, the pressure is external, with marriage-seeking singles pushing every potential friendship toward the "next level" or secretly wondering if every new friend is entertaining romantic notions. In other cases, the external pressure arises from friends, family, and fellow churchgoers—some well-meaning and some meddling—piling on conflicting questions, comments, and advice. This sort of pressure can crush budding friendships. It can raise false expectations where none had previously existed. It can be toxic to cross-gender relations in the Body of Christ. When faced with the question "Does the Church foster a culture in which men and women can be friends with each other?" many of those who responded *No* acknowledged this dynamic in their comments. The leadership of most churches, however, seem unconscious of it.

In his book *Sacred Unions, Sacred Passions: Engaging the Mystery of Friendship Between Men and Women,* Dan Brennan bemoans the fact that in Western culture, friendships between men and women are seen almost exclusively as stepping stones to romantic love. Between the sexes, friendship for friendship's sake is not recognized as an end in itself. If acknowledged at all, it's given so little value in society that it's often stigmatized with the word *just*: as in, "We're *just friends*."[1] What a shame. Friendship is too valuable to be thoughtlessly diminished. There is no *just* about friendship and support, especially between the sexes. In God's plan, men and women need each other, and not just as romantic partners. Women ministered to Jesus. Jesus ministered to women. Deborah and Barak worked in partnership. Aquilla and Priscilla supported Paul. I could go on, but that topic deserves its own book—which is no doubt why Dan Brennan chose to write one.

Brennan's book on cross-gender spiritual formation raises

some interesting questions. You might not agree with all of his conclusions, but you may find his thoughts provocative. On one of his points, however, I think we could all agree: "Within rule-driven, sex-segregated communities, the physical and emotional estrangement between men and women falls far short of moral formation and ever-deepening reconciliation."[2]

When men and women within the church become friends with each other, they are generally given the side-eye. Instead of recognizing their bond as a sign that God has redeemed and reconciled the sexes, people suspect the relationship. Adopting this attitude toward cross-gender friendship is akin to counting your broken eggshells before they've shattered.

Christ came to reconcile all of creation. Through the power of the cross and the ministry of the Spirit, He reconciles husbands to wives, children to parents, men to women, former oppressors to the oppressed, employers to employees, Jew to Gentile, bond to free, and all to Himself.

The Gospel slices through history, parting heaven from hell and unifying all Christ-followers under one banner. If the Gospel draws any divisions, it draws them between truth and error. It parts the sheep from among the goats, not the sheep from one another.

As brothers and sisters in Christ, we can show the world what true relations between men and women should look like. Instead of bowing to Freud's theory that all motivations are driven by sexual urges, Christians should stand united in the fellowship of true brotherly love. We do not flirt with sexual temptation. We are fully aware of the danger; however, we needn't assume it lurking around every relational corner.

In his book *The Four Loves,* C.S. Lewis acknowledges the temptation of *eros*—erotic love—in friendship between the sexes, and he addresses the perils with grace:

> When two people who thus discover that they are on the same secret road [of friendship] are of different sexes, the friendship which arises between them will very easily pass—may pass in the first half-hour—into erotic love. Indeed, unless they are physically repulsive to each other or unless one or both already loves elsewhere, it is almost certain to do so sooner or later. And conversely, erotic love may lead to Friendship between the lovers. But this, so far from obliterating the distinction between the two loves, puts it in a clearer light. If one who was first, in the deep and full sense, your Friend, is then gradually or suddenly revealed as also your lover you will certainly not want to share the Beloved's erotic love with any third. But you will have no jealousy at all about sharing the Friendship. Nothing so enriches an erotic love as the discovery that the Beloved can deeply, truly and spontaneously enter into Friendship with the Friends you already had: to feel that not only are we two united by erotic love but we three or four or five are all travelers on the same quest, have all a common vision.[3]

In an ideal situation, relationships outside of marital bonds should not be seen as competing loves but as complimentary ones. In this way, all friendship enriches the connection of romantic lovers. Note, however, that Lewis's statements on the benefits of friendship to romantic love are not unequivocal. He notes that "unless one or both already loves elsewhere," human nature will generally drive friendship toward erotic love. Marriage does not necessarily indicate a stable, loving relationship capable of rooting the affections. If the marriage bears strain, then friendship from an outside source may prove a vehicle for temptation.

We must also understand that not everyone is comfortable with the concept of cross-gender friendships. Clearly, discernment must be exercised, but the need for discernment doesn't mean cross-gender friendship outside of a marriage partner must be eliminated entirely.

Perhaps we might make some progress if we class cross-gender friendship under Paul's teachings on doubtful things as found in I Corinthians 8. In this passage, Paul addresses one specific aspect of Christian Liberty: whether or not a believer should eat food offered to idols. These principles have long been applied by Christians to any doubtful area of spiritual life. Therefore, if our friendship will offend a weaker believer, if our friendship will hinder the spread of the Gospel, if our friendship will threaten the personal spiritual life of an individual involved, then we must choose to abstain—not because the relationship is inherently wrong, but because its very existence could hinder those with less freedom in Christ.[4]

> We are so hypersensitive and paranoid about affairs and inappropriate relationships that men and women are hardly able to develop friendships at all. ... I think we'd probably have less trouble with affairs if we taught people how to be friends with members of the opposite sex and how to relate rather than promote a culture of fear and shame.
>
> ~ Rachel, Married

Personally, I've found it challenging that within Christian doctrine, the strong always accommodate the weak. Even within areas of understanding and doctrine, those who are strong are admonished to have patience with the weak—to comfort them rather than confront (1 Thessalonians 5:14).

On the surface, this principle may seem counterintuitive. In our current human system, strength leads naturally to power;

however, we must reframe this common understanding in light of the strength Jesus demonstrated during His time of incarnation. His strength often demonstrated itself through restraint. Our Savior stooped to conquer. Can we offer less?

Discussion Questions:

1. What are the benefits and pitfalls of encouraging cross-gender friendships within the Body of Christ?
2. How does our church body have room to grow in this area?

Action Points:

- Care for all single women as you would your own mothers and sisters: ask after their needs and help out where you can. If they so require, proactively help them with automotive issues; remember them when it's time to put up storm shutters; mow their lawns when you mow yours; shovel their driveways when you shovel yours; offer them a set number of handyman hours per year (when they use them up, offer more); make it clear that they can call your family in the middle of the night if they hear something weird on the roof or something scratching at the back door; invite them fully into family life.
- Care for all single men as you would your own fathers and brothers: ask after their needs and pitch in where you can. If they're helpless in the kitchen, bake them delicious meals, which you then divide into individual containers, stocking their freezers with home cooking; offer to teach them to cook, clean, bake or sew; issue open invitations to family game nights and children's birthday parties; invite them fully into family life.

CHAPTER 9

CAN'T WE ALL JUST GET ALONG?

In true extrovert style, while researching this book I discussed its topics with everyone I knew. Along the way, a close friend pointed out that relationships of *any* kind are hard—period. True friendship requires risk, time, energy, commitment, service, and sacrifice. We must willingly lower our defenses, allow others to know us, and be open to the possibility that this relationship will change us. True friendship reaps great rewards but poses great challenges. This seems especially true of friendships between marrieds and singles.

> [Marrieds'] lives are so different. I mean SO. And it's hard for them to lift their eyes from their roles of spouse/parent. It's hard to convince them that a 'single' friendship has benefits that go both ways. Hard to convince them that I want it and that they should, too. BUT I will say this: the few marrieds that I'm working on befriending now? That subject is so full of beauty, real Christianity, and tremendous dividends that it would take a few more paragraphs to explain.
> ~ Beth, Single

Such friendships need not be inherently problematic. With the exception of my younger sister, most of my closest friends are married. At my age, this situation is understandable. It doesn't bother me. My approach to friendship is this: if we're kindred souls, I don't care if you're male or female, young or old, single or married, human or alien, vegetable or mineral—we're going to be friends if you'll have me.

This mindset goes against the grain of many in the Church, especially the ones who seem intent on herding all the "single gals" together. Enforced social clumping didn't bother me so much when I was in my twenties, but now that I'm zeroing in on middle age, it's a different matter.

It's not that I don't love and appreciate young singles. Who else would explain to me how social media works? I'm as willing as the next person to befriend young singles, invite them over for coffee, counsel them, and mentor them. I love their enthusiastic idealism (even as I'm mildly annoyed by it), and I chuckle every time one of them tells me they want to be like me when they grow up. But to be transparent, spending lots of time with young singles makes me tired. They're eagerly launching forth, riding the first high crests of life; meanwhile, I'm sailing peacefully into the harbor of middle age, ready to drop anchor in a quiet cove and start thinking about who's going to take care of me if I develop dementia.

I do not avoid the younger generation. I really do love them, and given my penchant for early-onset geezerdom, I could use occasional doses of their breathless enthusiasm and incessant curiosity. But some balance is required. The only way I'm going to stay sane in my relationships is through also developing deep, close friendships with some of the women in my church who are my age and older.

That's not as easy as it sounds. Unfortunately, there are some barriers.

FRIENDSHIP BARRIERS

False Assumptions

Married people occasionally assume that singles only want to spend time with other singles, or that they only want to spend time with marrieds away from their kids.

If marrieds assume that singles will find spending time with children annoying from time to time, they'd be right. Marrieds know better than anyone how all-absorbing children can be. However, they shouldn't assume that marital status alone is indicative of whether or not someone has the desire or inclination to spend extended time around children. In fact, singles (not to mention marrieds who don't have children at home) may genuinely enjoy mixing it up with the kids—annoyances and all. In fact, they're less likely to be burnt out on tasks and conversations parents find tedious through constant repetition.

> Married friends with children tend to drop out of having a social life entirely. This can be frustrating.
> ~ Tom, Single

Speaking from personal experience, I appreciate having an outlet for my nurturing instincts, and my favorite friendships are formed around entire families. If I can become friends with both spouses *and* become a surrogate aunt to their children, I don't mind coffee over homework at the kitchen table or evening hangouts at soccer practice. I've become just as invested in the lives of some of my friends' children as I have in the lives of my own nieces and nephews. This has enriched my life greatly.

Many singles actively long for this sort of wholesale welcome into a family. Don't assume they only want to hang out with other singles or people in their own age/peer group.

TIME AND PLACE

If marrieds and singles seek meaningful friendships, they must overcome the barriers of time and place. Fortunately, the process is simple. We do not need to meet at a third-party location such as a restaurant or a coffee shop in order for our fellowship to be valid. Waiting for such perfect conditions is like waiting for lightning on a sunny day (more common than you might think here in Florida, but still rare enough to use as an example).

We need not equate "social life" with going out. It could mean that once a week, you invite friends with the same taste in TV over to your house to share some homemade snacks and watch a show together. It could mean that your single friend drops by for coffee on her way home from work in the afternoon. It could mean that the next time you start a long-term renovation project, you ask a single from your church to devote a few hours a week to help you out.

A living room, a garage, or a back porch—these backdrops are just as valid for relationship building as a night out—perhaps even more so. Sure, a bevy of screaming children reenacting the Trail of Tears in the living room doesn't provide an ideal framework for a heart-to-heart; but remember that you must overcome these same barriers in your married friendships (often served with a double scoop, since in that case, both of you may have children to contend with). The conditions for budding friendship may not seem ideal,

> I only find being friends with singles challenging because I can't give as much time to the relationship as I'd like.
> ~Jodee, Married

but less-than-ideal is better than no friendship at all.

Lack of Mindfulness

Many singles who took the survey said they did not feel so much discriminated against in church life as they felt simply forgotten—by pastors preparing the sermons and by friends caught up in the couple-centric, family-driven evangelical subculture. I know it's accidental, but neglect doesn't need to be purposeful in order to feel painful.

For the younger singles, once their peers couple up and start going on double dates and coupled activities together, they begin to feel like the social equivalent of a square-wheeled bicycle—clunking along through life, just trying to make relationships work however they can. Older singles trying to become part of a church family find making connections problematic, since the adults in their peer group tend to form their social lives around family-centered activities.

> It's hard to mesh our schedules, which sounds ridiculous, but it's true. I feel lame whipping out my calendar and saying, basically, 'I have fifteen minutes on March 3rd free.' This is probably my issue. I do wish that more singles in my area would reach out to us married folks, too.
>
> ~ Katherine, Married

One widower who took the survey, when asked if he had difficulty maintaining relationships with married couples, responded somewhat tellingly, "No. I was married for fourteen years, so the majority of my friends are married." The ingrained idea that marrieds would be friends with marrieds and singles with singles is inherent in his answer. Don't misunderstand; I'm so glad the friendships forged through the common bond of marriage and family have persisted through his bereavement and inadvertent lapse into singlehood. As well they should! It's just that his wording provided a reverse image of so many comments made by singles that it seemed prudent to note.

Inflexibility

All of us know at least one person who has lived alone for so long that independence has hardened into inflexibility. This sort of single, usually older, does not handle noise, chaos, or change very well and has very particular ideas about the "correct way" to do everything. At the first hint of Plan B, he or she stomps off in a huff. Integrating these seemingly-inflexible singles into family life is bound to be challenging, if not downright frustrating. It might even prove impossible, but you'll never know unless you try.

> There does tend to be a pattern where long-term singles become less and less tolerant over time of anything they can't control. I have often wondered if this "my way has to be the only way" attitude has caused the isolation, or is the result of isolation. Either way, that can become tedious.
>
> ~ Nathan, Married

This step requires patience and prayer—especially at the beginning—but an open-armed welcome into a family could become the best thing that ever happened to these lonely souls. Welcoming them into your family may require sacrifices on your part—sacrifices of time, patience, and personal preference. But what manner of ministry does not involve sacrifice?

I have one last caveat to offer. I say this not to offer an escape hatch but to temper idealism with a note of reality. It could be that some of the singles in your church suffer from a martyr-like, self-imposed loneliness. They have given in to self-pity and will refuse all attempts of help. If this is the case, a reaching hand might be able to pull them out of the mire: then again, they might push back and sink further into isolation.

Their reaction is not your responsibility. Willingness to reach out is.

Comfort Zones

> I think both single and married people need to stretch ourselves beyond our comfort zone. As a single person, why shouldn't I invite a family over for a meal? You should see the shocked faces when I've done that before.
> ~ Candace, Single

All share some responsibility in this area. Inflexible singles (or those moving unwittingly down the path to inflexibility) can stand to loosen up, and married people can learn mindfulness when it comes to including singles in their social agendas. Both groups could benefit from expanded comfort zones.

That's why both sides should strive to stretch hands across the divide.

CONCLUSION

When planning your social calendar for the month, be mindful of singles. Invite at least one to your dinners; make sure they know there's a group headed upstate for a camping trip; don't let them miss out on cultural events like plays and concerts because they don't have anyone to go with them. Personally, I don't mind attending events alone. I do not let the lack of a friend or date keep me back from something I want to experience, but that doesn't mean I consider the situation ideal. I'd much rather go with friends, which I try to do whenever I can.

Singles acknowledge the full-tilt busyness of family life. We know how hectic it all can be, but we also know how it feels to be invited along for the ride. If I choose to reject, my subsequent loneliness is my own responsibility. If I'm never given the chance to opt-in, it's yours.

Discussion Questions:

1. How can our church avoid enforced social clumping based on marital status?
2. What motivates singles and marrieds to congregate with their own kind? How can we encourage the two groups to come together?
3. What can we do to help break down the barriers keeping singles and marrieds from building strong friendships?

Action Points:

- Include singles in group dinner plans.
- Don't just double date with other couples. Involve singles in group activities.

> I live with my parents. One of the best aspects: I live with my parents. One of the worst aspects: I live with my parents.
> ~ Anonymous, Single

CHAPTER 10

THE GOOD, THE BAD, AND THE UGLY

Part of my survey asked singles to detail their home lives. I asked if they lived alone or with housemates and what the best and worst aspects of their living situations were. I wish I could cut and paste every survey response so that you could experience the same amusement I did as I read through them. Some responses were terse, while others rambled for pages of florid prose with plots straight from a cheap novel. I read bitter diatribes against annoying roommates and paeans of bliss regarding a home of one's own. However, there was a lot of overlap. To spare you the tedium, I've taken what I learned from my own personal experience as well as from the survey responses, poured it all into a giant pot, and distilled three basic brews: The Good, The Bad, and The Ugly. I've also compiled a list of practical solutions to help solve some of the singles' most common housing woes.

THE GOOD

If singles choose to live alone, their situation carries distinct advantages. For one, they have complete independence. Their time and money are their own, and they're free to prioritize these resources and invest them how they will.

For all intents and purposes, these singles come and go as they wish, completely unfettered by spouse or dependents. If they so desire, they may live the spontaneous life of bohemian vagabonds. At the first hint of wanderlust, they can take impulsive, all-night drives to the coast or go traipsing off to backpack Europe. They can participate in short-term service trips and help chaperone weekend youth group retreats. They do what they want, when they want, and how they want, leaving their married friends to pine over sun-drenched travel photos splashed across social media.

When they're not off trotting the globe, these singles enjoy the comforts of a home arranged to their exact specifications. They share a bathroom with no one. Whether they live in their own little house or in a snug studio apartment, they find it easy to keep everything tidy since they have no one to clean up after but themselves. Furthermore, they are able to manage their homes according to their own preferences, with changes requiring little to no lead time. Since singles can act as their own consensus, decisions are made without argument, debate, or compromise. When they feel that the time has come to re-do the kitchen, replace the drapes, or upgrade the toilet to a fancy Japanese model that gives massages and plays music, there's little need for hemming and hawing.

Best of all, plans can change with every whim. They will hear no complaints over last-minute shifts. Whenever they want, they can cancel home-cooked dinners in favor of takeout, the couch, and a good book. Their freedom doesn't just benefit them, however. If needed, they can drop everything and dash across town to help friends, family, and fellow church members who face emergencies.

Living autonomously as they do, these singles have been able to discover who they are and what they're capable of doing. Living alone has fostered independence and self-confidence. They've learned self-sufficiency, tenacity, and reliance on the fullness of Christ.

Unbound by the constraints of child-rearing (in most cases), singles who live alone can set aside large chunks of time to focus on spiritual matters: reading, studying, meditating, giving, and praying. They have a unique opportunity to seek God first, both with their daily use of time and with the general ordering of their lives. They have great freedom to serve and commit to church work. It's easy for them to arrive at events early to set up and stay late to clean. The Church is blessed to have access to people with so much time and energy.

Their flexible timetables don't just benefit church work. They can also reach into the broader community. They're able to take time for self-care, reading, hobbies, friends, continuing education, discipleship, mentoring, sports, the arts, and exploration. They're able to accomplish life goals and chase down dreams without major distractions or guilt. They can develop the sort of close, intimate friendships that married people don't always have the time or emotional energy to pursue.

The peace and quiet that living alone affords cannot be understated. With little to no sleep interruption, singles are able to stay relatively fresh and well-rested. Nobody rouses them in the middle of the night with their snoring. Nobody wakes them up in the pre-dawn hours by running toy cars over their faces. Nobody shouts questions at them through bathroom doors. They can leave for church as soon as they're ready since their shoes are the only shoes they need to keep track of.

Singles who live with housemates not only enjoy the advantages already mentioned, but they also benefit from additional perks. Housemates provide a measure companionship and accountability. With someone else to share the expenses, singles don't feel they're operating without a financial safety net. Housemates can drop each other off when the car's in the shop, share in the housework and bring greater feelings of safety at night. Plus, there's someone else around to help eat the fresh fruit and leftovers before they go bad. While close relationships don't always develop among housemates, when they do, such bonds can help mitigate the loneliness that sometimes overtakes singles.

Living alone and sharing with housemates aren't the only living options singles enjoy. Some men and women choose to continue living at home with their families. If relations with parents and siblings are good, the situation affords many benefits: greater security, increased financial stability, relational warmth, and a caring support system. The reciprocal benefits for the family can be great as well. Younger siblings enjoy another adult presence, while older parents gain companionship and helping hands.

THE BAD

Singles who live alone find many downsides to their situations. Coming home to an empty house at the end of a long day is demoralizing, not to mention potentially creepy for those who have active imaginations or are easily spooked. Unless singles maintain a packed schedule, there's nothing to do and nobody to do it with. The lack of companionship can be crushing. Enduring trials or illness alone further flattens the spirit. These singles live with the constant awareness that if they fall and hurt themselves in the shower, nobody will miss them for days.

With little to no accountability regarding how they spend their time and money, they're tempted to blow their savings on huge entertainment systems or extended island-hopping jaunts to the South Pacific. Although they could spend their money more wisely, they suspect that if they don't seem to be "enjoying" the overt advantages of singleness, there will always be someone on hand to accuse them of being mopey and static. Then again if they do, they could be seen as trapped in an extended, irresponsible adolescence that only the responsibilities of marriage and family could cure. Since the entire situation is a Catch-22, they might as well err on the side that puts stamps in their passports.

Not that singles know nothing of responsibility. With no one to share household chores and financial burdens, *everything* becomes their responsibility: the house, the car, the cooking, the cleaning, the laundry, the shopping, the repairs, the bills. There's no one to help run errands, pick them up when the car's in the shop, or lend a hand moving furniture or putting boxes in the attic. While most singles aren't incapable of doing these things, these tasks are much less onerous when shared. Singles know friends and family would help, but sometimes it's wearing to feel that they're always going around asking for help. It's hard not to feel like a burden.

Since they bear full household responsibilities, singles actually may find it more difficult to give financially and commit themselves to church work. Without a partner to help them juggle bill-paying, errand running, home and auto maintenance, and other such tasks, they may have less expendable time and money than their pastors and married counterparts assume they do. When their time and financial constraints run contrary to expectations, singles may find themselves facing spoken or unspoken judgment for not fully "devoting their singleness" to Christ.

Without the built-in companionship of a spouse, they must

muddle through big-picture decision making alone. With no one consistently on hand to help either validate or troubleshoot ideas, they're left to chase down advice from anyone who will sit still long enough to listen to their problems.

Although singles are masters of their own castles, each kingdom is a modest one with its own problems. Empty houses are lonely. Cooking for one is impossible. Being sick alone is the worst. Singles who live independently lack companionship, intimacy, emotional support, and physical touch.

More time spent alone means more time for prayer and personal study; however, singles still find developing Christlikeness a challenge. Since they rarely need to consider the thoughts and feelings of others, there's little chance to live sacrificially. Without a daily companion with whom to walk through life, they're not able to gain necessary feedback on their daily habits and decisions, meaning they can lack the impetus to grow and change.

While lying alone in the dark on their narrow beds, they may struggle with fear for their safety, every sound heralding the arrival of thieves and rapists. Sexual temptation is also a problem. Thwarted passions and frustrated longings intensify over time; however, because sexual temptation and lust carry a social stigma within many spiritual communities, singles don't always feel comfortable asking for counsel or prayer in this matter, even from their closest church friends and trusted mentors.

Depending on their personality types, singles who live alone might struggle with overwhelming feelings of rejection, isolation, and self-pity.

Housemates aren't always the answer, however, and that option holds its own pitfalls. Although housemates mitigate isolation, finding compatible ones isn't always possible. Often singles are forced to settle on someone who is not ideal in order to lift the financial burden. The trouble is, having a housemate with whom they can't connect only leads to increased feelings of emotional isolation. If the single doesn't get along with housemates, feeling comfortable at home is virtually impossible. Also, the conflicts of the house can add a measure of guilt. Already emotionally isolated, having issues with housemates can give singles unreasonable feelings of personal failure—perhaps even depression. Furthermore, living long-term with housemates can leave singles feeling forever stuck in dorm-life, with their roommates becoming increasingly younger as they themselves age. This situation often leads to lifestyle instability, as roommates move through their own life stages and move out, leaving the single to start again with someone new.

Compounding the situation, older church members tend to think of younger unmarried church members as college students. The housemate-situation does nothing to dispel this perception. Single men especially find it hard to keep their homes from feeling like frat houses, especially since their kitchens often lack big-ticket cooking items and the sort of expensive appliances young couples generally receive as wedding presents or housewarming gifts. (I met one single man who asked a female colleague to help him decorate his new home so that it *wouldn't* look like a frat house.)

The final option, living with family, has its own specialized difficulties—not to mention potential for major drama. Singles who continue to live with their families may find relational issues from childhood carrying over into adult life. Aging parents can become increasingly difficult housemates, offering their adult children little personal freedom and making demands on their time and attention that housemates would never do—and singles living at home may find themselves reacting irrationally to minor inconveniences. I say this to my shame. After four years of college and a year living on my own, I moved back in with my parents for a while. During that time, I was overly sensitive to their questions about my plans (did they not realize I was an adult?) and comically exasperated when asked to chip in with chores and household errands (did they think I was still in high school?). While I wouldn't have balked at picking up the occasional jug of milk for a roommate or keeping housemates apprised of late-night comings and goings, somehow relating to my parents in this way sent me around the bend. I'd like to think that with a few years behind me, I'd respond more reasonably now; however, perhaps parents and children will always struggle through extra layers of subtext. One thing seems consistent: even when the dynamic works well, singles living at home battle societal perceptions. Some assume all adult children living at home are mooching off their parents while others quietly shake their heads in silent judgment that these children have somehow failed to launch.

Single parents living on their own face further challenges. Many of them bear an almost crushing sense of responsibility. They must work to support the family, and yet working can interfere with having enough time to nurture their children. No matter how hard they try, they're falling short somewhere. Further, they're uniquely alone. Single parents have no one with whom to share childcare, with whom to talk through parenting problems or to back them up on discipline issues. And a social life? Unlikely. And that's no simple matter. A lack of meaningful interaction with other adults can have far-reaching repercussions. Years of communication with preschoolers and younger children can have a deep impact on a single parent's social ability, sense of value, and self-image; not to mention that a lack of meaningful dialogue with other adults often intensifies problems that might otherwise seem insignificant.

THE UGLY

While all aspects of single living have positives and negatives, the greatest possibilities for ugliness arise when singles live alone.

> I grew up in a loud Italian home. It was a lonely fact every day to eat alone at night. I would call people all the time while I was eating. Plus, trying to cut recipes in 4ths was rough. Everyone thought [I] should just get take-out or eat ready-made food. It was a reminder of awkwardness. It's a not a very deep answer, but it was a bitter pill to swallow. I enjoyed getting together with non-threatening singles to hang with and eat with, without fear or pressure to "like" anyone.
>
> ~ Mimi, Married

At its best, single living can teach total reliance on Christ. At its worst, it devolves into total self-absorption. Even as they long for companionship and spiritual correction, many singles living alone grow increasingly proud and isolated. Prolonged indulgence of their own wants and desires leads to self-interested habits that will strain all relationships.

With no one else's thoughts or feelings to consider, singles become so accustomed to doing as they please that almost unknowingly, they chafe when not granted their own way. With no one to draw them out of their comfort zones, they're increasingly cut off from new people and experiences. Many fall back on social media to bridge the emotional gap, but online interaction cannot replace human connection. With no one sharing their lives, singles could struggle with feeling purposeless. Some fall into deep depression.

> For a single trying to live a God-pleasing life, I think the hardest thing to deal with is sexual desire. It's something people are wired for and it's natural, but especially as one gets older, it can be really hard to not have a way of fulfilling that desire. Obviously, a single shouldn't feed this desire in unhealthy ways like watching pornography, which would only make it harder to deal with the desire without it being fulfilled in God's way. But other than not feeding it, and working hard to trust God, I am not really sure how a single person can make this aspect easier to live with.
> ~ Rebecca, Married

Extroverted singles lack someone to talk through their day with, while introverts experience tension between their desire for alone time and their need for support. With no one to "corner" them as a coach does a fighter in the ring, both introverts and extroverts lack the advantage of an outside set of eyes. They need an encouraging voice to cut through the fight, telling them when to get up and keep slugging and when to tap out.

For the single Christian living alone, managing sex drives while living alone poses exceptional challenges, and a total lack of accountability leaves us open to a wide array of temptations. Apart from the ease with which they could invite someone into their beds, they have nearly unfettered access to pornography and other sexual possibilities via the internet. While singles living alone are by no means the only group in the church struggling to swim against the culture's sexual rip current, their situation makes them uniquely vulnerable to its pull.

> Singles have a gift of time and quiet which, if left unchecked, can lead to loneliness and self-pity but when viewed in light of the gospel this time can be used to further Christ's kingdom in a variety of ways.
> ~ Anonymous, Single
>
> 
>
> I do not believe that isolation and individualism are Biblical concepts. We are called to live in community. For a single person, I do believe that living in community is going to lead to much more fruit and completeness than living alone. I would encourage all single people to seek out a living situation that allows them to be in community.
> ~ Anonymous, Married

THE SOLUTION

"It is not good for man to be alone." For this reason, God created Eve and Adam as a pair (Genesis 2:18); and for this reason, He continues to set the lonely ones in families (Psalm 68:6). As discussed in a previous chapter, this biblical concept exists in tension with American culture, a culture that favors autonomy over community. Although marriage is certainly grounds for forming a new home around a newly-created family (Genesis 2:24), there's nothing that says adult children must do so just to prove their independence and value in society. Could it be that by adopting the world's mindset toward adulthood, we've created a situation in which singles feel forced to cut themselves off from the very sort of community and fellowship they need?

This situation can be tempered as singles intentionally seek intimate community for themselves, building a pattern of coexistence and actively seeking to attach themselves to families. We have numerous examples of singles living communally in Scripture—with Christ acting as our primary example, as He does in all areas. Jesus lived with His family until He began His ministry at age thirty, at which point He commenced traveling with a group of twelve men (plus a coterie of helpers and hangers-on). Based on what's recorded in Scripture, He barely had another moment alone until His body was in the tomb. Likewise, Paul, often touted as the Bible's most prominent single, doesn't seem to have spent much time alone. He stayed with Ananias in Damascus; traveled with Barnabas, John Mark, and Silas; lived and worked alongside Priscilla and Aquilla in Corinth; lived with Philip the Evangelist in Caesarea; and shared countless hours with cellmates and guards during his many imprisonments. Paul and Jesus were singles, yes, but they hardly ever spent prolonged time alone. How can we encourage more Christian singles to emulate this sort of lifestyle?

> My experience is that singles are seldom proactive about attaching themselves to families: moving in with them, going on vacation [with them], adopting kids like nephews and nieces, etc.
> ~ Jonathan, Married/Church Leader

There could be several reasons why singles aren't as proactive in this area as they should be. First, we've already established that communal living goes against the fabric of American society. Second, any attempt on the part of a single to attach to a family without an expressed invitation could prove awkward. Third, even if singles actively desire inclusion in a family, they might have trouble finding a good match. Much like any relationship dynamic, there must be affection and "comfortableness" on both sides in order for the arrangement to work.

If the singles in your church aren't proactively building community for themselves, consider making their needs a specific area of personal ministry. Instead of sitting back and wondering when they're going to build community themselves, step into the gap on their behalf. This is what Christ did for us. It is the Gospel in action.

Rather than merely hinting that you're ready to meet singles halfway, take active steps to meet them where they are, even if this requires more time and effort than you expected. Don't just invite them to sit with you in church: go sit with them. Invite them over to your house repeatedly; take them out to eat; include them in discussions of upcoming vacation plans. A trip together could be a good trial run to see if living in community is an option. Above all, be consistent about your efforts to build a real relationship. In this way, you'll demonstrate the image of Christ.

Before you were formed, God knew you. Long before your birth, Jesus satisfied your sin debt on the cross. Previous to your awareness of your need, the Holy Spirit opened your eyes to salvation. Nothing that you've gained can be attributed to you; it's all been granted through the mercy and love of your Father. In the same spirit, we don't wait for the needy among us to seek to meet their own needs. We step forward in mercy and love, ready to serve them through the power that God provides.

"This is my commandment, that you love one another as I have loved you" (John 15:12).

If we're going to love as Christ loved, we'll need to learn sacrificial living.

Sometimes lonely people, in an effort to prove that they're not wasting their lives, wind up with schedules more packed and frantic than their child-rearing counterparts. While a full schedule isn't a sin, and some singles experience packed schedules due to God's direct leading, those who pursue busyness as an avenue for personal fulfillment will miss the mark. While busyness temporarily assuages loneliness, it can't erase it.

Ironically, busyness is often what distracts us from investing the time and energy needed to cultivate the deeply rooted relationships needed to practice real community and discipleship. Naturally, there are some seasons during which life sets the pace. Rearing small children, caring for a seriously ill family member, launching a business, establishing a new ministry—such periods of intensity don't allow for much else. Apart from such situations, however, we must carve out time to pursue relationships with our brothers and sisters in the Body of Christ.

Although all three groups (singles, marrieds, and church leaders) bear responsibility in bridging this gap, for the purposes of our discussion, we will focus on the particular struggles faced by singles socializing in a partnered world.

SINGLES SOCIALIZING IN A PARTNERED WORLD

Although socializing in a partnered world can be challenging for singles, there's no room here for self-pity or blame-shifting on either side. We must seek to extend further grace to one another in this area. From your end, you can start by initiating an open dialogue with your single friends on this topic, seeking to draw out their perspectives, listening for what you can do to fill in any gaps. Remember to listen with an ear toward helping rather than toward refuting their experiences.

Open dialogue works best when the listener has a teachable spirit and a closed mouth. When the single begins sharing, listen fully before you comment. Lecturing them mid-answer will do more damage than not asking their opinions in the first place. If you develop the habit of listening, you may be surprised at what people will tell you freely. Once you know where people are coming from, you will understand how to meet their needs more effectively.

> I dislike it when other singles complain about being "left out" in the church. Married people could often say the same thing since it's up to each person to plug themselves into the church, not for the church to reach out to grab them. If you put yourself out there and get involved in the body of the church, you'll find a place to serve and be needed.
> ~ Bethany, Single

PRACTICAL WAYS TO BUILD COMMUNITY WITH SINGLES

- Don't leave the burden of initiation on the singles. Default toward outreach.
- Know that almost overwhelmingly, singles cited loneliness as the number one downside to living alone. Even for the ones who are happy and content in their singleness, it's a serious problem. Anything you can do to mitigate their loneliness would be a wonderful investment of your time.
- Temper your suggestions that a pet will solve all loneliness problems for the single. As one survey-taker put it, "My dog is sweet, but he just wags his tail."

- If you're able, adopt a single as your own. Pray for him, feed him, care for him, encourage him, challenge him, mentor him, and love him.
- Guard against comparing living situations: "You're so lucky/blessed to have so much free time/peace and quiet/independence." We understand that when you make these offhanded comments you're really lamenting your own lack of those items; however, be sensitive to the fact that for some singles, these situations do not feel "lucky" or very much like "blessings." Then again, other singles revel in these aspects of single living—so use your discretion. (I know one single who, when faced with a version of this comment, just singsongs "Liiiiiife choicessss" and gleefully moonwalks away. When such comments are offered to me, I just smile. Despite occasional bouts of loneliness, I make great use my time/peace/quiet/independence. And the Lord puts me to work. You likely wouldn't be holding this book in your hands if I didn't have the life I have right now.)
- Allow singles to admit a level of dissatisfaction with their situations—only in this way can they become proactive about improvement. If any mention of discontent is shut down with the "you need to be content with your singleness" speech, you only pile guilt on top of discontentment. It's possible to feel discontent with certain aspects of single life, but it does not follow that this discontent equates immediately with dissatisfaction in the goodness of God. We all face situations like this. Case in point: while I was researching this book, my dad was diagnosed with cancer. I'm not ashamed to admit that I was dissatisfied with the diagnosis. I didn't want him to be sick. I mourned his illness and hated the fact that sin has

corrupted the perfect human system that God initiated at Creation. I'd much rather my father were healthy and strong than sick and suffering; however, my dissatisfaction with my father's cancer does not equal doubt in the goodness of God any more than a single's dissatisfaction with her single state is an inherent spiritual weakness.

- Encourage the fostering of relationships among all generations in the church. In this way, older members become mentors, younger members become surrogate children, and peers become brothers and sisters. In order to act as a real Family of Christ, we need all of these relationships to be functional. When the Christian family functions correctly, everyone benefits—especially the lonely. Even more importantly, it is the supernatural character of Christian brotherhood that sets the way of Christ apart.[1] In the South, American Christians have not lost the distinction of calling one another "Brother" and "Sister"; whether or not they actually treat one another as a family is another matter. Demonstrating the powerful unity of real spiritual brotherhood, unified under the care of our Father and the leadership of Christ, our lives and relationships become a powerful witness to the world.
- Move from open-ended offers to specific ones. Don't just invite them over "whenever." Designate a weekly meal or game night. Don't just offer handyman help "whenever." Schedule time in advance and then follow through.
- Encourage co-housing with families. Although not all singles would be open to living with a family, some would jump at the chance. Remember that God has promised to set the lonely ones in families (Psalm 68:6); this is true of the

outcast, the refugee, the marginalized, the poor, the friendless, the widow, the orphan, and the lonely single. Be open to the possibility that you could become one of the families in which lonely ones find a place. When we were alone, the Spirit sought us out; Jesus prepared our home, and the Father adopted us. As we develop in Christlikeness, we model this process. As He loved, so we love (John 15:11-12).

- Support Christian communal living. Unfortunately, since the great theological split between Protestants and Catholics, Protestants have allowed communal Christian living to fall by the wayside, associating it with only with monks and monasteries. Communal living, however, is modeled for us in the Book of Acts. Communal living is about more than just being housemates. It's about Christians living together and seeing themselves as more than rent-splitting partners, but as spiritual partners, offering one another care, accountability, support, fellowship, and love while simultaneously learning to serve one another.

> Mostly I live alone, but a few months of the year I have housemates. The best aspect about having housemates is if I choke on my vitamins they will be there to help me. The worst aspect about having housemates is having to worry about encroaching on each other's personal space. Like walking into the bathroom when someone is already on the toilet.
>
> ~ Bethany, Single

- Don't make your single adult children feel that they need to leave home in order to operate as fully-functioning adults with a measure of autonomy.

- Know that for single parents, it's a struggle to get things done with young children in the home. Even something as simple as picking up the kids and taking them to the park once a week so that the parent can clean the house without interruptions (or pay bills or study or take a nap) can be of huge assistance.

A FINAL NOTE ON HOSPITALITY

Married respondents and church leaders mentioned frequently in their survey responses that singles are just as responsible to be hospitable to families as families are to be hospitable to them. While I applaud the egalitarian approach and agree in spirit, I need to offer some caveats. If you mean that singles should give and receive invitations, bring food to church potlucks, and not constantly refuse to engage in church life while still actively complaining of loneliness, then I agree. But the burden of hospitality for singles can't always equal that of married couples and families.

While this is more a matter of financial ability than singleness, logically a two-income family would be able to feed one extra person more easily than a one-income single can feed a family. For example, if a family invites me over for Sunday lunch, they need only add one to what they're already planning: one extra chair, one extra place setting, and one extra serving of dinner. Most people can handle adding one without feeling as if they're making much of a stretch. However, if I invite a family of four over to my house, I must add four: four chairs, four place settings, four servings of dinner. I don't even own four chairs. I currently live in a six-hundred square-foot studio apartment with a tiny kitchenette, one chair (not counting the sofa), and limited cooking options. Having a family over simply isn't practical for me. I could always invite the family out to a restaurant, but I can't afford to pick up the bill for an entire family very often, and inviting families out to eat in a "let's go Dutch" way without knowing their budget restrictions isn't considerate.

For single parents, the situation is even more tricky. Single parenting is almost hopelessly expensive, and hospitality isn't cheap. So that's an added complication. Not to mention the fact that most single parents find themselves overwhelmed just trying to keep up with daily life; they don't have a lot of room for the planning required to exercise hospitality. Your invitation can be a huge blessing and comfort to them during a time when they feel most abandoned.

For these reasons, I believe that the ministry of hospitality in the church should be encouraged primarily among married couples and families. This is just as true for reaching out to singles as it is to older couples in the church who live far from their children and grandchildren. These lonely church members (or, I should say, potentially lonely) should be the main focus of our inreach.

ONE LAST CAVEAT

A common theme of this book is that not all singles have been created equal. This concept is borne out in how this chapter is applied. As I read through the survey responses, I came across a single who remarked, "Living alone gives me space to process my day." Of course, I find that the exact opposite true for me. When I'm alone, I miss having someone to talk to at the end of the day.

Each single in your church will have unique wants based on personality, temperament, and living situation. Treat individual needs individually. Listen, share compassion, meet needs.

Discussion Questions:

1. Which aspects of single living could pose the greatest spiritual challenges? Which ones could provide the greatest opportunities for growth?
2. How might introversion and extroversion affect how singles cope with living alone?

Action Points:

- Remember that most singles have never had wedding showers or housewarmings. If needed, shower them with gifts for the home.
- Take care of them when they're sick. Being sick alone truly is the worst.
- Do what you can to offset high expenses. For example, watch for BOGO deals on food items that you know they like; then buy one for yourself and pass the other one along.
- Remember that singles lack physical intimacy. I'm not talking just about sex, but warm hugs, pats on the back, and hand-holding. Regular physical touch can increase immune function, decrease production of the stress hormone cortisol, and lower blood pressure and heart rate. Hugs also cause the body to release oxytocin, a hormone that further lowers stress and promotes human bonding; while handholding has been proven to positively affect people's ability to withstand pain.[2] Many singles cannot benefit from any of this. Obviously, there are limits to how this touch-deficiency should be addressed (and by whom), but being aware that singles lack human touch can influence your interactions with them. While I was researching this book, my friend Becca suggested that churches initiate a Hug Ministry. While I can't get away from how inherently creepy that

sounds, I can't say she's completely wrong. (Note: Please don't start spontaneously bear-hugging singles this coming Sunday. People have differing levels of comfort regarding touch and personal space. Be tactful as you figure this one out).

CHAPTER 11

WALKING IN A DATELESS WONDERLAND

"I just want you to be happy," is the worst thing someone could say to me concerning my singleness. I often feel like people think that I am unhappy being single and that is why they make efforts to set me up. I am content in Christ and I don't like that the church thinks you are incomplete if you are not married.
~ Courtney, Single

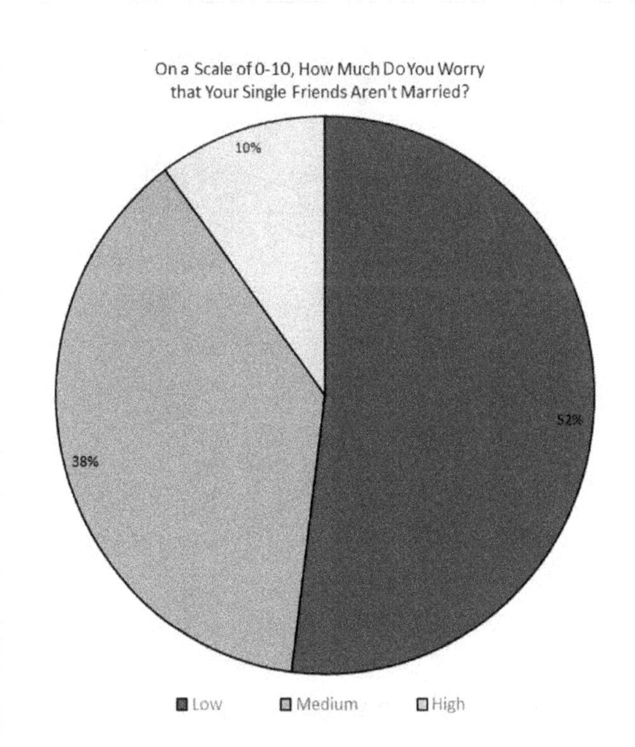

If you study the chart above, you'll find that when marrieds were asked to rate on a scale of 0-10 how much they worry about their single friends not being married, 10% admitted to worrying a high amount (7-10), 38% reported a medium amount (4-6), and 52% a low amount (0-3). When you take a look at the numbers turned in by the singles when asked a similar question, however, an interesting trend emerges.

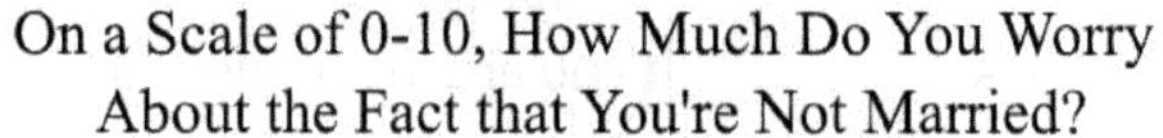

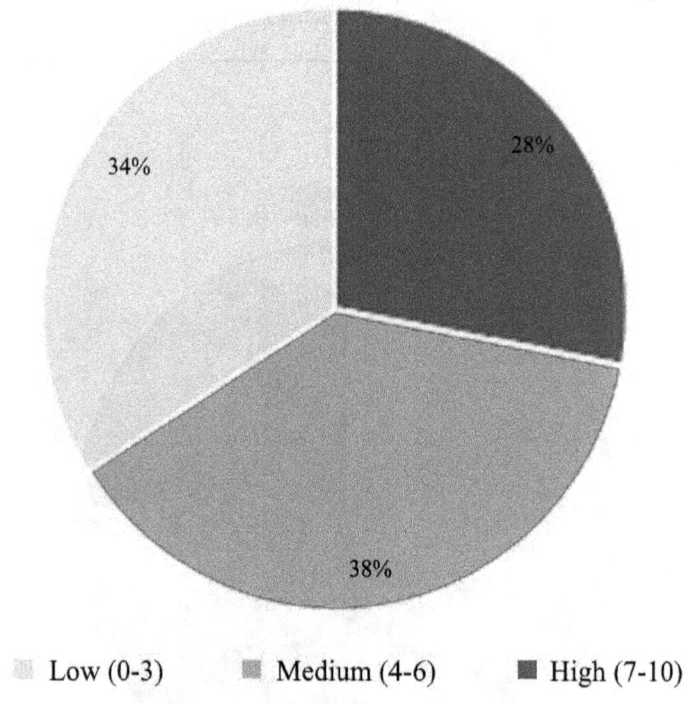

Interestingly, singles on the whole report a higher level of worry about their lack of a spouse than their married friends worry on their behalf. This result surprised me. I fully expected the numbers to show that singles' friends tend to worry about the question much more than the singles themselves do.

Most of the singles I know complain that everyone in their life, from their parents to their pastors to their friends, are "way more worried" about their marital status than they are. Either 1) I've been talking almost exclusively to outliers, 2) people on both sides of the divide gave answers that don't match perfectly with their behavior, or 3) something else is going on.

As for the third option, I have a theory. We'll get to it. First, we have some foundational ground to cover.

TO EACH HIS OWN

> Married people don't seem to get that I'm perfectly happy being single. That doesn't mean that I'm against marriage or that I plan to always be single. It's just that I'm not as desperate to get married as they are to fix me up with a man.
> ~ Anonymous, Single

With the rise of selfie culture, we have more opportunities than ever to become experts on our own faces. In many cases, we know our appearances so well that we can actually feel alarmed when we see a non-reversed image of our own face.[1] We're so used to seeing mirrored images that we come to believe the flipped version is our true appearance. Since we're accustomed to seeing reflected images, we don't really look how we think we really look. Although we see ourselves in the mirror every day, other people have a much clearer idea of what we truly look like, because they see our true image rather than our mirrored one. Additionally, while we tend to focus mostly on one view of ourselves (the front), others see us easily from all sides, noting embarrassing oversights (and hopefully, if they're true friends, discreetly notifying us).

Both our faces and our lives take on different appearances

depending on the perspective from which they're viewed.

MARRED IMAGES

Though created in the image of God, we are nevertheless twisted by sin, our attention constantly curving toward ourselves. This narcissistic tendency affects how we process our relationships. Writing in *Psychology Today,* one psychotherapist says, "Relationships are transactional, but because we are generally not reflexively altruistic societally - in other words, we tend to operate from the primally-wired 'It's all about me!' - we typically tend to see only our own side of the equation, and often to our peril."[2]

Our me-centered hard-wiring overrides almost all other considerations, necessitating real effort to see life from other's perspectives. Unless we make a conscious effort to do so, we are in danger of literally becoming our own gods—of creating our own worlds and values.

Because the unregenerate mind is self-driven, we cannot imagine (in our own strength, at least) that anyone could possibly be happy apart from what has made us happy; therefore, singles report that our married friends remain unconvinced that we could ever be happy without a spouse, regardless of our protests to the contrary.

My sister-in-law and I illustrate this phenomenon perfectly. Dawn married my brother straight out of college. She's been a wife and mother for twenty years as of this writing, and she loves the whole package. Her personality uniquely suits her to wife-and-mother-hood, and she can't imagine a happy life without her husband and family. She's told me that she also can't imagine living my life.

Do you want to know a secret? I feel the same way. As full of love and warmth as her situation is, her lifestyle allows little autonomy. For as much as I admire her exertion and unflagging energy on behalf of her family, I suspect that her life would choke me just as mine would dissatisfy her.

In His wisdom, God blessed each of us uniquely with the personality traits and skills needed to face the life He's planned for us. I recognize that Dawn does not feel stifled by her life, and she recognizes that I do not feel afraid or isolated in mine. Naturally, since we know one another quite well, these assumptions are not difficult to overcome.

I wish all singles could say the same of their married friends, some of whom assume that since *they* would not be happy or fulfilled without a spouse, *we* cannot be either. In their minds, we're either lying about our underlying contentment, or we're fooling ourselves.

Only Christ can help shift our ego-driven perspective to an others-driven one. Christ, who entered fully into the human condition, learned the feel of sorrow, temptations, anguish, and pain; we must ask for His help to see life through the eyes of others—not to judge them (for even the Son of Man came not into the world to condemn the world—John 3:17) but to lead them to the Shepherd who offers a more abundant life (John 10:9-10).

Real abundant life comes not through any human relationships but through an increasing knowledge of the Creator God who made us and longs for us to find our completion in Him.

THE QUESTION OF PRESSURE

In the introduction to this chapter, I referenced a theory I had regarding why singles feel that their married friends are worried about them. The theory goes like this. It's only natural that singles would worry more about being single than their friends would worry for them. After all, they're the ones actually experiencing the situation, whereas their friends might only think about their concern from time to time. As one of my married respondents wrote regarding whether or not he worried about his unmarried friends, "Why should I worry about that? I can't marry them."

And yet all singles know that some of their married friends worry about them. They know because a few of their married friends bring up the issue more than the singles themselves do. This, in turn, leads singles to assume that their friends must be thinking about it more than they actually are.

According to the data, however, not only do marrieds worry about singles *less* than the singles assume they do, most singles worry *a bit more* about their marital status than they are letting on. Despite singles being worried about the question of a potential marriage (a combined 78% admit to Medium-to-High worry levels), they have the tendency to interpret any sort of encouragement on this subject from their married peers as pressure.

I designed one of the questions in my survey to test this hypothesis. With every other question, I was very careful to use the same wording for both the singles and the marrieds; however, for this question, I used slightly different wording for each group. As you can see, for each one, I selected heavily connotative words.

To the marrieds, I asked: Do you *encourage* your single friends to date? To the singles, I asked: Do your married friends *pressure* you to date? My theory was that the data would show that from the perspective of most singles, encouragement feels like pressure.

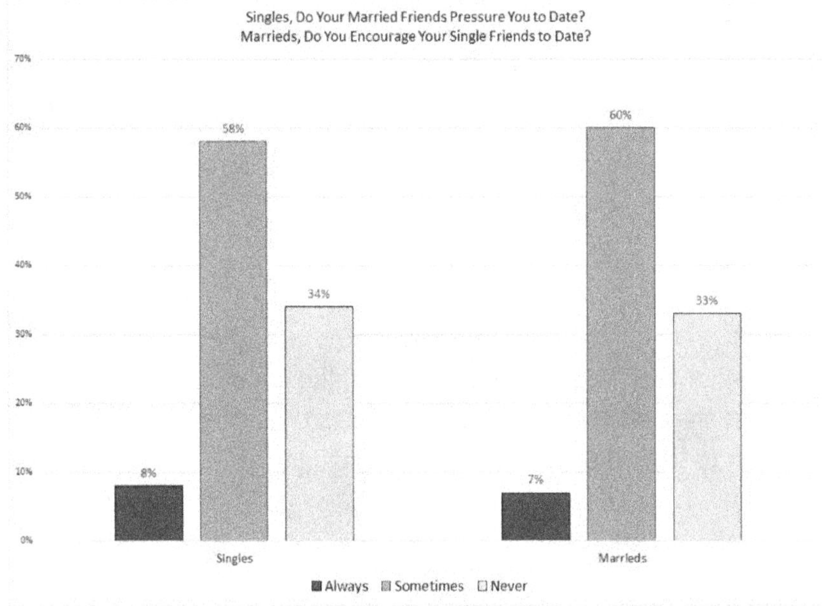

There are always exceptions to the rule, but according to the data, my theory proved surprisingly accurate. With nearly identical percentages weighing in on both sides, the numbers suggest that singles tend to interpret encouragement as pressure, whether it's intended as such or not.

So, what are we to take from this? Should you stop encouraging your single friends to date—even the ones who actively seek to be married? Should you take your hands off the situation to mitigate the risk of annoying a single?

Not at all. Read on.

WHAT THE DATA IMPLIES

The Good News

The good news is that singles aren't necessarily opposed to set-ups. Frankly, this data point surprised me because I hate set-ups with the heat of a thousand suns, and I fully expected all my fellow singles to back me up. Upon a closer reading of the comments, however, I realized that while most singles aren't opposed to set-ups from trusted friends, they *are* opposed to *awkward* set-ups with *incompatible people* forced on them by *well-meaning acquaintances*.

> I don't want my single girlfriends to date for the sake of dating. I am not going to personally encourage a spirit of dissatisfaction with the place God has them in right now. I will listen to their hearts and pray accordingly.
> ~ Hilary, Married
>
> 
>
> I really haven't been set up at all. Sometimes I feel like that would be nice. Or if families in the church would do more mixed people dinners without being obvious about set ups.
> ~ Anonymous, Single

The Better News

The data also reveals that while singles are sometimes annoyed with you for trying to set them up (and while some of them are *always* annoyed with you for trying to set them up), even the annoyed ones still appreciate your concern. Many expressed in the comments that their annoyance stemmed more from the methods than anything else.

The Best News

The best news is that using the wrong method to set people up can be easily remedied. So listen up, my would-be matchmaking friends. I'm not going to tell you to stop trying to help your single friends find suitable spouses, because if we can't look to people in our churches to help us, whom can we trust? Instead of trying to stop you, I'm going to help you learn to do it right. Once you're doing it right, you'll cut down on a lot of needless pressure singles experience during set-ups.

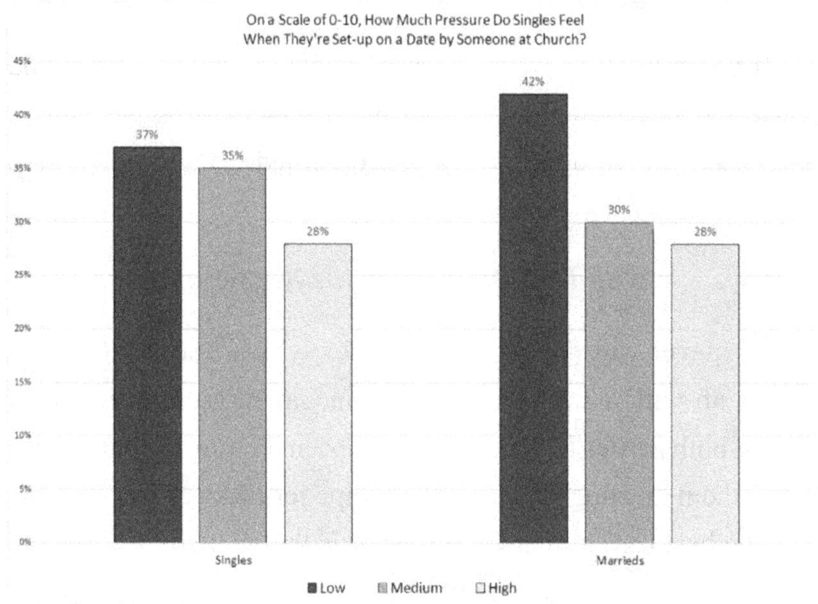

HOW TO PULL OFF A SUCCESSFUL SET-UP

STEP ONE: KNOW BOTH SIDES

First, resign yourself to the fact that two awesome people won't always form an awesome couple. Second, know that if—within ten minutes of being introduced to a single—you say something like, "I have a nephew who's still single, too. You would just love him!" you've undermined your credibility. A standard rule of thumb: the better you know both sides of the equation, the better the chances that your set-ups will work out.

Set-ups work best when you know both people well enough to

judge shared interests, compatibility, and spiritual sensitivity. Strangers only see the surface. Friends know the patterns of our souls. Knowing someone well qualifies you not only to identify your friend's "type" with increased precision but will also keep you from trying to enforce a set-up on someone who doesn't want one.

If you truly desire to minister to singles by helping them find mates, the first step should be to build relationships with them. Only after you've done so are you qualified to proceed to Step Two.

Step Two: Mitigate Awkwardness

Whatever you do, don't hit singles with a Sneak Attack by turning up with a surprise introduction, saying right out loud in front of both parties how much you've been looking forward to the two of them meeting. That's just a recipe for awkwardness.

The best-case scenario for set-ups is that you *don't set up the couple at all*, thus alleviating much potential awkwardness. Ideally, the non-set-up could be as simple as inviting them both to the same group event. By ensuring that they'll appear in the same space together, you've provided a chance for them to notice each other on their own in a low-risk atmosphere.

In the event that a non-set-up set-up is logistically impossible, a few simple questions may be all it takes to get the ball rolling:

1) Are you interested in meeting someone?

2) Would you mind if I shared your email address/phone number with him/her?

But remember, if you're going to ask these questions, you

must be ready to take no for an answer.

Step Three: Take No for an Answer

We know by now that not all singles have been created equal. As a natural result, not everyone actually desires to be set up, no matter how seemingly-perfect the match. Your refusal to take no for an answer can not only create a rift in your relationship with singles but also demonstrate a lack of empathy and no lack of pride. Despite your conviction that an ultimate marriage is in the making, the singles themselves are the ones making the choice.

Bear in mind that even when you ask careful questions first, you still might not get the full story. Perhaps the person you're engaging in the set-up is single because she's recovering from a difficult divorce. Maybe he has a complicated family situation he doesn't want to explain. What if she's suffering the after-effects of sexual abuse and has decided not to date until she's reached a more appropriate level of healing? What if he's dealing with same-sex attractions? What if she comes from a cultural background with distinctive family expectations of courtship and marriage, and she's seeking to honor her parents throughout the process? Attempting to force a set-up without knowledge of underlying issues will get you nowhere, and your insistence will likely lead the single in question to avoid you.

If, however, the singles in question do agree to a set-up, rejoice! It's time for Step Four.

Step Four: Hands Off

Do what you can to get them together; then be ready to take your hands off the situation. Clarify from the outset that (barring anything drastic), you will not let the outcome of the potential set-up damage your friendship with either side. Let the two meet and then accept or reject one another without any further meddling. If the relationship doesn't work out, let it go.

If you have made mistakes in this area in the past, don't beat yourself up. Instead, determine to progress with increased sensitivity next time. We do not enter this world as experts—nor will we leave it as such. The best we can do is to learn as we go.

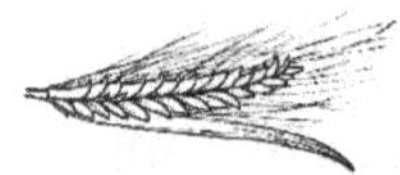

Discussion Questions:

1. How might we truly encourage singles in finding compatible spouses?
2. In what ways might encouragement feel like pressure?

Action Points:

- Pray for wisdom in helping your single Christian friends find one another.
- Plan some non-pressure-inducing meet-ups for like-minded singles.

> Unsolicited comments about singleness are almost always 'insensitive.' Not intentionally, I'm sure, but indicative of how misunderstood and unaccepted the long-term single can be.
> ~ Anonymous, Single.

CHAPTER 12

ON GIVING ADVICE

I would love to say that the best advice I've ever received on singleness came from my married friends. I can't. What I can tell you is that my married friends have offered me the *most* advice about being single.

Toward the end of my survey, I thought it might be fun to ask singles to share some of the least-helpful advice they've been given over the years. I understand it wasn't fair of me to weight the question this way, but I thought the answers might prove illuminating when compared with the advice I solicited from married survey-takers. Sure enough, there was some overlap.

Below you'll find some of the most common responses from singles. The unhelpful advice is in quotes, and any commentary offered by the survey takers themselves is included after that.

WHAT'S THE LEAST HELPFUL ADVICE YOU'VE BEEN GIVEN?

- "Stop looking for your true love and they will find you." This is totally unhelpful.
- "You just need to focus on God, and then I bet your husband will come right around the corner."
- "Just date more."
- "Lose weight, and they will come."

- "When you stop looking for love it will happen." I didn't look for love, and I was intensely focused on faith, school, and work for ten years without any blip on the love radar.
- "You ought to get out there and look around!" I did.
- "Just pray harder and get skinnier."
- Being told I "just need to get out there more" adds no value, especially when coming from friends who married high school sweethearts or others who have no experience dating in the last 3+ decades.
- "Stop looking. Raise your standards. Lower your standards."
- "Why don't you just get out there and find someone? Be proactive!" You know, because finding a good single guy when you're in your thirties is so easy.
- It's frustrating hearing from married friends who are ladies who tell me that I'm such a nice guy, they don't understand why I'm still single.
- "If someone decides to 'take you on,' don't turn him away."
- "Maybe the reason God hasn't given you a spouse yet is that He's waiting until you develop this one character quality."
- "Have you tried internet dating?" I don't like being asked if I've tried internet dating because I have, and it didn't work, and it made me depressed and stripped my self-worth.
- "It's not too late! I know someone who was married at fifty-eight!" In other words, cheer up—it's still possible that you're not a *complete* loser.

- "It'll happen once you're content."
- "You need to move to an area with more people."
- "It will happen in the right timing. God will bring that person along." [It's] cruel to inspire false hope about something about which you know nothing. You can't know that it will happen.
- "You will find someone when you aren't looking." Ugh! I'm always looking, so that's never going to happen.
- "Just look at this trial/experience/struggle as preparation for when you're married."
- "Just relax and it will happen." I've been relaxing for eight years.
- "Singleness is a season. We all go through it. Just use that time to prepare for The One."
- "When I was 23, somebody said to me I was not following God's plan for my life. Otherwise, I would have been married."
- "Some people have been single longer than you." Who cares? Are those people me? No.
- [They offer] reassurance that being single is okay as if I didn't know it was.
- "You must not *want* to find someone because you haven't done ___________."
- "You should get a boyfriend." Oh, right. I'll just go right out to the boyfriend store and pick one out this afternoon. Why didn't I think of that?? I'm so glad you're here to help me with these things.

While some of these comments are obviously cringe-worthy,

others may sound innocuous to you and leave you wondering if all singles are just over-sensitive. Regardless of your reaction, I'd like to discuss several of the most common ones below, expanding on what exactly makes them so problematic for singles.

PROBLEMATIC ADVICE

"Stop looking and you will find love." / "It will happen when you are content."

While encouraging others to wait on the Lord is certainly appropriate, it's never a *passive* waiting. Paul does not admonish followers of Christ to wait for people to ask about the Gospel. Instead, we are to preach the Gospel actively. This command does not ignore the act of the Holy Spirit in calling the lost to salvation; it's made possible *because of* it. We work, for God is working. This is true not just in evangelism but in all other areas of Christian service, church growth, and spiritual development. Because we know God is at work, our confidence in His effectiveness allows us to share in what He's already doing. Waiting on the Lord is not a passive experience. It's a time of prayer and active seeking to match our efforts to God's active will.

I see nothing to hinder us from applying the principle of active waiting to the development of personal relationships. If God has given a desire for Christian marriage—which according to Hebrews 13:4 is an honorable desire—then there's nothing to stop us from working toward that end while cooperating with the overruling work of our Father.

In this light, "waiting" for a spouse has less to do with inactivity and more to do with maintaining the right spirit throughout the process of actively seeking a mate. In all else we do, we wait for God to move—but we wait actively. We wait while we work, and we work while we wait, doing all to the glory of God and trusting Him with the results. As a church, we're active as we wait to be reunited with our Bridegroom. So, let's actively wait to be united with earthly spouses.

Pastors, teachers, youth leaders, and parents should take the lead on defining what it means to wait on the Lord for a spouse—especially for young adult church members, whose entire outlook will be shaped by the messages they absorb during these formative years. Just as we are active about helping them establish practical plans for a good education or a career path, we must become ambitious about helping them pursue strong Christian marriages.

We must begin with fostering relationships among Christian singles within Christian fellowship. In some cases, this might mean facilitating non-awkward set-ups. In other cases, it could mean removing the stigma around online dating. Singles of my own age group (Generation X) don't really consider online dating problematic. Several of my good friends met wonderful spouses online. My friends in the Boomer generation, however, tend to view the entire process askance. I actually witnessed an older woman I know roll her eyes during a discussion about a mutual friend meeting her spouse online. The fact that the man was fresh-faced, wholesome, and a dedicated Christian seemed to matter less to her than how the two met. I find this mind-boggling.

People who disparage online dating tend to believe that it's a quick fix for impatient singles. They seem to believe that if only singles were a little more patient and content, God would bring "The One" in time. It's hard to imagine applying similar logic to gaining college acceptance ("Don't work so hard on your college applications—it just makes you seem needy and desperate. Trust

God and let the college acceptances come to you!") or finding a fulfilling career ("The right employers will come if only you're patient and trust God enough!"). Since neither the biblical record nor common sense back up this sort of thinking, we can only wonder why so many people tacitly accept it.

"Some people have been single longer than you."

The single who contributed this quote already implied that this comment adds very little value to the conversation. Imagine you have two friends who have both broken a leg. It takes one friend six weeks to heal and the other eight weeks. Now, do you say to the friend in a cast for six weeks, "You have no right to struggle; after all, Betty has been in a cast longer than you"? Of course, we wouldn't say that (unless we wanted to get smacked in the head with a crutch). Being in a cast is terrible, and if you haven't experienced this particular form of torture, you are fortunate. Knowing that someone else has to wear her cast longer than I do won't actively make my situation easier. I still won't be able to shower easily, drive myself places, or carry a cup of coffee to the kitchen table by myself.

As someone who suffers chronic physical pain, I've found great sympathy in the ranks of other sufferers, and I've never had anybody claim that my pain isn't valid because it's less intense. While we can be inspired by those who suffer more deeply than we do, our experience of suffering is in no way diminished simply because theirs is greater. Likewise, just because someone has been unhappily single longer than I have (or has had a harder emotional struggle through the process), that does not mean I will automatically stop suffering.

When I was in my early twenties, a friend gave me some wise

advice. Pain isn't something to compare, she told me. God has not called us to someone else's pain: He's called us to our own. The hardest thing we've ever been through is still our hardest thing. Your journey may inspire others, and theirs may inspire yours, but your hardest experience is your hardest experience.

We haven't been called to compare struggles; we have been called to bear one another's burdens (Galatians 6:2). Therefore, when helping friends who struggle with the more difficult aspects of singleness, acknowledge their pain.

"You need to change [x] about yourself."

God created each of us with unique talents, interests, tastes, and senses of humor; and what makes us unique makes us special. At least, that's what we're told when we're young. At what point does the narrative shift from "be yourself" to "be someone else in order to land a spouse"?

When someone is told to change [x], unless the [x] in that equation is an actual sin, the advice is both demoralizing and counterproductive. Every time a man is told he needs a better car to find a wife, he will think of happily married men who drive clunkers (or who don't have any cars at all). When a woman is told she will never find a husband as long as she's so intimidating, she will think of all of the competent, self-assured women she knows whose spouses love them for their assertiveness. Introverts need not become extroverts, nor vice versa. Fashion blind men need not receive a makeover to land a wife.

As Christians, we understand that the question is not whether we can be ourselves but whether we can be like Christ. Any change we encourage should be one that brings us closer to His image, not closer to an image of whatever the current trend might be. We must never stress change for anything but the glory of God. Any other reason cheapens the process of sanctification, making holiness about us rather than about Him.

"MAYBE THE REASON GOD HASN'T GIVEN YOU A SPOUSE YET IS THAT HE'S WAITING UNTIL YOU DEVELOP THIS ONE CHARACTER QUALITY."

Someone fairly close to me used to say this, and although I tend to give people the benefit of the doubt and assume they don't mean to be hurtful, I could only let this go for so long. After hearing that perhaps God wasn't giving me a spouse because I wasn't patient enough or caring enough or gentle enough, I could no longer let these comments slide.

This comment sets up marriage as a reward, establishing it as the carrot God dangles in front of us to motivate us to change. This view of marriage relates closely to tenants of the Prosperity Gospel, a false theological framework that encourages Christians to remain faithful in order to secure financial security or material blessings from God. Within the Prosperity Gospel, not only must Christians give generously in order to receive compensation from God, but they also view faith as a self-generated spiritual force that leads to the "blessings" of prosperity. If we buy into this brand of faith, we don't do the right thing because it is the *right thing.* We do the right things in order to *get* the "right things."[1]

These teachings crumble in the light of the true Gospel. We serve a Savior who laid it all down—His glory, His will, His life. In return, we give because he freely gave Himself to us. By the same token, we do not change in order to receive something tangible from Him. As the Holy Spirit reveals truth to us, we change into His image, bringing Him delight.

Further, the idea that God's withholding a spouse until I've "earned it" just doesn't bear true in the lives of most married people. If that's really how it worked, then the Christians who marry young would all be spiritual giants.

Remember, marriage symbolizes the Christian's mysterious union with Christ. If we viewed marriage as a reward for good behavior, our entire understanding of salvation would shift. Of necessity, we enter our spiritual union with Christ broken, because only through union with Him can we be made whole. If we had to fix ourselves in order to deserve a spouse, what would that say about our union with Christ? Must it, too, be earned?

Yes, it's true that high moral fiber and strong character will make us better spouses and therefore presumably more attractive for likeminded believers, but it does not follow that God reserves marriage for the spiritually mature. In many cases, marriage becomes the crucible through which maturity is made possible.

"Just look at this trial/experience/struggle as preparation for when you're married."

This comment closely relates to the ones listed above, but I thought it worth mentioning if only to point out a few dangerous underpinning ideas. First, this comment assumes we'll all be married eventually. As we've already discussed, that's just not the case. Second, it feeds the unhealthy holding-pattern mentality to which some singles have unfortunately fallen prey. While looking ahead toward marriage as the time when their adult lives will *really* start, they overlook today's opportunities for growth, service, and joy. I've known women who have put off travel or Christian service opportunities because that's something they want to do one day "with a husband." I currently serve as a part-time nanny to five children. I work with these Podlings daily and care for them full-time when their parents are out of town. While I'm with them, I have full responsibilities and have experienced most of the annoyances accompanying parenthood, including interrupted sleep, late-night vomit sessions, useless debates about food, fingers poking under the bathroom door, and apocalyptic bath sessions.

I've lost track of the times people have told me this is great practice for when I have my own kids.

> In regards to advice, I would just say that if someone has dating advice, they should always, always ask if you'd like to receive advice. Unsolicited dating advice, especially from people who got married young, can make me very frustrated. What I always find more helpful is honest dialogue about challenges, and when a person asks me how they can support me.
> ~ Anonymous, Single

Don't misunderstand; I'm not lashing out against kindly-meant offhand remarks. I'm trying to encourage us all not to trivialize the work in front of us by reducing it to the idea of "practice." Perhaps taking care of the Podlings *is* preparing me for a future family of my own. Then again, maybe not. Either way, I don't consider caring for these kids as preparing me for the as-yet-arrived "main point" of life. Right now, it *is* one of the main points. This work meets a need right now and is important in its own right. As such, I should take it seriously regardless of what the future may or may not hold. Important lessons and tasks should never be reduced as possible preparation for some future "main thing." Whatever is in front of us right now *is* the main thing. To see it as anything less is to devalue the task God's entrusted to us today.

"YOU NEED TO MOVE TO AN AREA WITH MORE PEOPLE."

This advice cheapens the role that strongly-built community plays in the life of the believer. The underlying message is that when pitted against one another, the hope of romantic love naturally trumps all other aspects of life: family, friends, church family, community roots, career, and so forth. Along with the recommendation that singles switch churches in order to find other Christian singles, the recommendation to move in order to meet potential spouses directly contradicts biblical teaching on fellowship and unity. Besides, given the general lack of accountability already inherent in the unmarried state, it's not always wise to encourage singles to voluntarily abandon their (often hard-won) support systems.

WHAT SHALL WE SAY, THEN?

The internet seems riddled with posts telling us what we're allowed to say and not say to one another. A quick search will reveal a flurry of posts with titles like "What Not to Say to the Moms of Preschoolers" and "How Not to Talk to Friends with Cancer." Although posts like this are helpful to a point, after a while, this attitude becomes a bit wearying. We're told what *not* to say and do but are not always given alternatives for how to help.

What, then, are we to do? Sit on our hands with our lips zipped shut while we watch our friends march in an unbroken line down a doomed path? Certainly not.

We all need help. Singles need help. Newly-marrieds need help. Parents need help. Teens need help. Men need help. Women need help. Families need help. Seniors need help. Pastors need help.

God charged us to proclaim His truth outward to the world and inward to one another. If we hold back from doing so for fear of alienating or offending, we deny our spiritual gifts and biblical responsibilities. We also deny the great benefits of deep fellowship. Says German theologian Dietrich Bonhoeffer:

> Where Christians live together, the time must inevitably come when in some crisis one person will have to declare God's Word and will to another. It is inconceivable that the things which are of utmost importance to each individual should not be spoken by one another. It is unchristian consciously to deprive another of the one decisive service we can render to him.[2]

In Ecclesiastes, Solomon reminds us that there's a time for everything. In addition to there being a time to be born, a time to die, a time to laugh, a time to mourn, a time to cast away stones, and a time to gather stones together, there's surely a time for giving advice. It's important to note, though, that there's also a time to *refrain* from giving advice.

Not every single is unmarried for lack of advice—good advice, even. Most situations are more complex. Then again, some may be in need of guidance and, based on the surveys, are actively seeking it—so we can't just write off giving advice completely. Even then, not every single in need of advice needs to hear it from *you*. Or it could be that God has placed you in this person's life at this unique time for this purpose. If this paragraph sounds contradictory, I apologize. My purpose isn't to be confusing but to encourage a nuanced approach. Naturally, each circumstance is different and requires prayer and discernment.

If we've discerned that the time for giving advice has come, and that we are indeed the best people for the job, what's the next step? In many events, the next step may actually be a step back.

FOUNDATIONAL RELATIONSHIPS

> I think married people find it awkward to talk to singles. They generally end up either complaining about their marriage or are trying to marry us off with Joe Schmoe. The other part is that they want to pry into our single life... [M]arried people have no problem inquiring in detail about who we are dating, etc., but if [we] probed into their sex or financial life like that, they would be offended.
>
> ~ Anonymous, Single

In order for advice to be effective, it must be rooted in some recognizable authority. For this reason, you would probably take the health advice of a fully-licensed medical practitioner over that of a professional birthday clown. Apart from the authority conferred by personal experience and advanced degrees, there is also an authority rooted in personal relationships.

Take, for example, the foundation my good friend Jodee uses to advise me.[3] Jodee may not be an authority on relationships in any professional sense, but she knows the Word, and she's definitely an authority on me. While Jodee and I didn't hit it off immediately, what started as weekly chats over coffee slowly morphed into true friendship. We started working out together, sharing book recommendations, studying the Bible together, going for "family" meals, and even taking some very memorable international trips riddled with hijinks and hilarity. We're so close now that I sometimes have to remind myself that our friendship is still fairly new in terms of years; but what we lack in length, we've made up for in depth, entering fully into each other's lives, not sparing the unsightly bits we are sometimes tempted to withhold from others out of pride or fear. We've been privy to some of each other's best and worst moments. A highlight reel of our friendship would read much like the opening lines of Charles Dickens's *A Tale of Two Cities*:

> It was the best of times,
> it was the worst of times,
> it was the age of wisdom,
> it was the age of foolishness,
> it was the epoch of belief,
> it was the epoch of incredulity,
> it was the season of Light,
> it was the season of Darkness,
> it was the spring of hope,
> it was the winter of despair,
> we had everything before us, we had nothing before us…[4]

And so forth.

Because we've endured so much together, Jodee can now say pretty much whatever she likes to me. No matter what it is, I'll take it.

Why?

1. Jodee loves. Because she loves me, she's careful with my emotions, even when confronting me about sin and foolishness. Undergirded by Scripture, that love provides a solid foundation for spiritual and relational advice.
2. Jodee listens. She doesn't just listen in order to turn our conversation into a counseling session (although sometimes that happens). She listens in order to understand. This understanding provides more basis for her advice.

3. Jodee knows. With few exceptions, right now Jodee knows me better than anyone else. For this reason, she won't give inapplicable advice. Her comments won't come out of left field but will speak to where I am and what my struggles are.

4. Jodee cares. She's not some random stranger bellowing that I should get married. Jodee has my best interests at heart. Because I trust her, I have faith that what she's telling me is for my own good, even if I don't like hearing it.

If you want to be heard, first listen. After you've listened, you'll not only know how best to approach the topic in a personal and private way, but you might even discover that the advice you felt so keen to offer is either off base or unnecessary.

The bottom line is this: if you don't feel close enough to the single in question that you'd enjoy him grilling you about your marriage, then you're not close enough to ask him probing questions or drop off-the-cuff personal advice.

Speaking from my own experience, this hasn't been too much of an issue with the people closest to me, who treat my singleness almost as a non-issue. Apart from helping to meet needs, I've clearly expressed, and occasionally extending tactful offers of set-ups, they pretty much just let me live my life. It's people who don't know me well who seem the most concerned, being pushy about dating and acting as if my unmarried state is an outrage akin to the Cuban Missile Crisis.

If the singles in your life were sorting you into these two groups, where might you find yourself?

Take a moment for some personal evaluation. If you don't

have any relationships with singles that go beyond the acquaintance stage, ask yourself why. Do you not know any singles? Is your church devoid of singles? (If so, there may be a reason.) Is potential friendship with singles simply not on your radar? Have you ever considered intentionally extending companionship and community to a single—for his sake as much as for yours? Have you tried and been rebuffed? Are you waiting for someone else to make the first move?

After you've built a supportive relationship through which you can effectively speak truth to one another, be sure that what you say is biblical, solid, rational, helpful, and loving.

> If I'm directly asked for advice, I will [give it], but it's going to be specific. There's no advice I'd give anyone without plenty of listening first.
> ~ Jacob, Married

I conclude this chapter with wise words from my married friend Jacob, who has never—to my memory—offered me any weird advice.

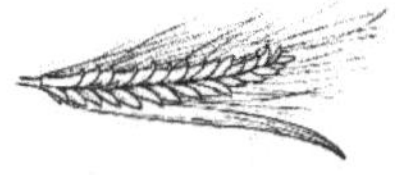

Discussion Questions:

1. How does relationship building aid in discipling, mentoring, and giving advice to singles?
2. In what practical ways can we be ambitious for the marriage of our single friends?

Action Points:

- Initiate an honest discussion with your single friends regarding the status of their relationships (or lack thereof).

- Formulate a practical plan to assist marriage-seekers in your church.

CHAPTER 13*

THE SPACE BETWEEN

We would be remiss if we didn't spend a moment thinking about those caught in the space between: those who are neither married nor technically single. Some people don't even consider these people "single" in the strictest sense because although they are still unmarried, they consider themselves taken. In reality, their situation carries great instability.

While some of the more conservative elements in the evangelical movement would say that "Christian dating" shouldn't exist, it does; and because it does, we must acknowledge that fact and discuss relevant considerations.

Pressure

Just as long-term singles complained about their church friends pressuring them to date, dating couples cited feeling immediate pressure to marry. In their survey responses, they expressed the desire for support and discipleship in the area of developing relationships; yet at the same time, they found themselves fighting expectations that they immediately march down the aisle and begin producing adorable Christian babies.

*While much of this chapter will address dating and engaged church members, some aspects will also apply to two groups detailed in Chapter 1, the Divorced Singles and the Functionally Single.

I experienced this phenomenon in my own early dating relationships. When I was in my twenties and just on the cusp of a new relationship, I brought my then-boyfriend to visit the church where I'd grown up. He hadn't been in the building for ten minutes before one of the senior members of the congregation approached us, took our hands, and joined them together under his own. "Dearly beloved," he intoned, patting our hands as he solemnly began the traditional wedding vows. This young man and I were neither mature enough nor comfortable enough with our new relationship to take something like this in stride. I don't remember how we responded. I hope it was with grace. I remember quietly imploding inside. For a time, I dreaded bringing another guy to church for fear that something like this would happen again. (To the credit of my church family, it hasn't.)

Again, most of these shenanigans circle back to the lack of foundational relationships. The man who performed the fake wedding didn't know me very well, didn't know my boyfriend at all, and didn't know the status of our relationship. Anyone who knew us well enough to know whether or not we would get a kick out of such a joke would have known that it wouldn't have been a good idea at the time.

Place

Often couples who meet and begin dating through a church singles group find that once they marry, they must transition into a different phase of church life, losing the relationships and community they've built. We should ask ourselves if enforced class separations based on marital status are worth the potential fallout.

PARENTS

If your adult children live with you or attend church with you, allow them the freedom to be adults. Give them space to date (or not to date) and freedom to pursue relationships without the fear that a breakup will cause undue fallout—barring catastrophic situations, of course.

Not every relationship will lead to marriage. Some associations are ultimately successful because they end before reaching the altar. Some are successful because through them, both partners take needed emotional or spiritual steps. We must stop seeing every "failed" romantic venture as an actual failure. Our desire for our loved ones should be for whatever outcome will best glorify God.

Sometimes what will most glorify God is a dating relationship leading naturally into a strong Christian marriage. Sometimes what will most glorify God is the couple recognizing that they would not suit. If the relationship is dysfunctional, if either side harbors doubts, or if major sins come to light early on, pushing forward toward marriage merely on the grounds that the couple has already made a commitment is unwise.

During the course of preparing this book, I was told the story of a Christian couple who had been having problems in their marriage. During counseling, the man admitted to his wife that he didn't think they were compatible. When she asked how long he'd felt this way, he said since before the wedding. However, because he'd already initiated the physical aspect to their relationship during their courtship, he didn't feel comfortable ending the relationship despite his doubts.

Although we will discuss Christian purity culture more fully in a moment, it's important to note at this point that in some ways, the careful boundaries Christians draw around the physical aspect of dating relationships can come with side effects, such as staying committed to problematic relationships by allowing the physical factor to trump all other considerations.

This potentially-messy aspect of relationships between the sexes must be appropriately addressed in all its fullness by pastors, church leaders, teachers, parents, and mentors. Dating couples in the church need a safety net of wise, loving counselors ready to help them navigate these issues with grace and discernment.

Creating a healthy environment for relationships to form and flourish is just as important as fostering an environment in which relationships can end when appropriate. Such an atmosphere will eliminate a lot of fear and provide confidence for potential Christian daters—not to mention help eliminate potential shipwrecked marriages down the line.

Purity

The topics of sexual temptation and frustration made frequent appearances in the comment section of my survey. Since none of my questions dealt directly with sex, I found the frequency of these statements quite telling.

Our ultimate relationship with the One who made us has been fractured by sin. As a result, we feel a constant sense of loneliness and are driven to seek spiritual, physical, and relational intimacy. God created the sexual aspect of marriage to express the mystery of spiritual union. It's only natural that men and women made in His image—whether believers or not—desire this sort of closeness. In Flannery O'Connor's posthumously-published prayer journal, she discusses this dynamic in unequivoqual terms.

> Man's desire for God is bedded in his unconscious [and] seeks to satisfy itself in physical possession of another human. This necessarily is a passing, fading attachment in its sensuous aspects since it is a poor substitute for what the unconscious is after. The more conscious the desire for God becomes the more successful union with another becomes because the intelligence realizes the relation in its relation to a greater desire [and] if this intelligence is in both parties the motive power in the desire for God becomes double [and] gains in becoming God-like.[1]

The struggle to maintain spiritual, emotional, mental, and physical purity is taxing for most singles, the majority of whom have not volunteered for a life of celibacy; instead, they find it forced upon them through a sustained delay in finding a marriage partner. Singles need help with handling their sexual urges, yet in most churches, frank discussions of sex and sexuality are rare—and in many cases, unfortunately, nearly taboo.

Christian leaders do speak to the importance of training men and women to keep themselves pure; but by that, they generally imply that singles must stay sexually pure "for marriage" by maintaining virgin status. This line of reasoning has a long track record in the evangelical movement, but it's actually flawed. Purity involves much more than refraining from a sexual act outside of marriage, and we do not keep ourselves pure just for the sake of a future spouse. When Jesus addressed the Pharisees on matters of adultery, he took the conversation from the act to the intent of the mind and heart (Matthew 5:27-28). If our version of purity entails only not having sex outside of marriage, then we can do everything but the act itself and still be considered "pure" by church standards—although not, of course, by biblical ones.

The argument that we must stay pure "for marriage" is also problematic. Not every Christian will marry—not even the ones who actively desire to do so. If we see maintaining purity as entering into some sort of mystical *quid pro quo* with God, what happens if we don't marry? Has it all been for nothing?

Popular evangelical purity culture misses the point entirely. Before we discuss what purity really is, however, we must discuss what purity is not.

PURITY IS NOT INNOCENCE

Mistaking innocence for purity can lead to disastrous consequences, especially in the way we raise our children and prepare them for whatever future they might face. Although some Christians are of the opinion that there's no such thing as "too sheltered," they fail to grasp that sheltering does not inevitably produce purity. It leads to innocence—which is not in itself a bad thing but is certainly not the same thing. When God placed Adam and Eve in Eden, they were innocent; but when the chance for sin came, their innocence did not save them.

PURITY IS NOT MORAL CONFORMITY

Mistaking outward moral cleanliness for real purity fails to protect the spot where sin really begins—the heart. Many Christians (both single and married) consider themselves sexually pure because they've not actively participated in sex outside marriage. Jesus reminds us, as He always does, that it's in the heart where the real sin takes place. If purity and moral conformity were the same things, Jesus would have been best friends with the teachers of the Law. Instead, He called them hypocrites (Matthew

23:27).

Real Purity

Real purity is best understood through Jesus' words in Matthew 5:8: "Blessed are the pure in heart, for they shall see God." Pure hearts allow the Spirit free reign. A strong work of the Spirit in our hearts fuels a closer relationship with God, allowing us to see Him more clearly. Telling the pure in heart that they shall see God is safe, says C.S. Lewis, because only the pure in heart wish to do so.[2] A clearer view of God leads to a further recognition of our sinful condition, which in turn leads to an increasingly purer heart, which leads to a stronger work of the Spirit. This dynamic furthers every sort of purity—including sexual purity.

Progeny

Children conceived outside marriage are a natural biological result of sex—and a gift of God no matter the circumstances (Psalm 127:3). Scripture records many examples of God working through the lives of men and women who resulted from unplanned pregnancies. Children resulting from incest, seduction, prostitution, and adultery all appear in the direct line of the Messiah. What a gracious God—to demonstrate through His Son how sin can be redeemed for His glory.

Sexual sins, like any other sins, are atoned by the blood of Christ through repentance. Any wish to rush a couple to marriage for the simple reason that they have had sex and/or produced a child must be tempered by the understanding that marriage is a serious commitment not to be undertaken lightly and that extramarital sex and the conceiving of children outside of marriage are not atoned through marriage.

THE PATH FORWARD

Rather than skimming the surface of singles' sexual struggles, let's deal with their roots. Believers of all ages must be vigorously, lovingly discipled—encouraged to grow and change from the inside out. Only by focusing on matters of the heart, as Jesus did, can we hope to effect actual change.

Therefore, instead of focusing on "tricks" to keep dating couples from being alone together; instead of simply falling back on telling them to flee temptation; instead of inventing arbitrary rules about whether or not Christian singles should date or touch or hold hands or kiss before the wedding, let's first evaluate what such methods actually teach.

Yes, instruct singles regarding the rewards of practicing chastity, but frame this conversation within the greater awareness of who God is and what sort of total purity He expects from us: spiritual, emotional, mental, and physical. Don't trivialize sex by treating it as a bargaining chip for a potential future happy marriage. Yes, warn men and women of the fallout of the hookup culture, but root this discussion in good theology: that deliberately going against the express will of God damages our relationship with Him and keeps us from knowing and more intimately loving Him.

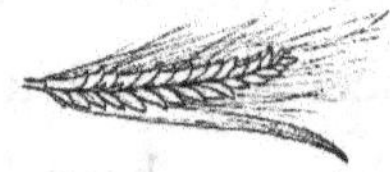

Discussion Questions:

1. What pressures might couples dating inside the church face that couples outside the church might not?
2. In what situations should singles who have had sex

and/or produced a child be encouraged to marry one another? When should marriage not be encouraged?

Action Points:

- Create a church culture in which issues of sex and sexuality can be discussed and are fully addressed theologically.
- Remember that although my survey did not directly address issues of sex, survey-takers often brought up sexual temptation in the comment section. Foster a church culture that is open and honest about matters relating to human sexuality. Christians should not be embarrassed to talk about sex. God made sex, and the right practice of sexuality reflects His glory. Says John Piper, "Sex is made for the glory of Christ — for the Christ-exalting glory of covenant-keeping faithfulness in marriage, and for the glory of Christ-exalting chastity in singleness. It is always good. Sex is always an occasion to show that the Giver of sex is better than sex."[3] If you're a mentor or spiritual leader, prayerfully prepare to counsel biblically in matters of human sexuality, sexual temptation, and lust. This isn't just a problem for the guys, either: make sure the female leaders in your church are likewise equipped. Finally, be sure to articulate a biblical approach on matters of homosexual practice, same-sex attraction, and transgender issues within the church. If we cannot discuss these matters within the bonds of Christian fellowship, where can we turn to discuss them?
- Encourage physical fitness. Even Paul admitted that bodily exercise has some minor benefits (1 Timothy 4:8). Sometimes this verse is quoted as a reason *not* to exercise, but the fact that the benefits of physical fitness are minor does not mean they're not worth pursuing at all. Since we're more likely to give in to temptation when we're at physically low points (hungry, tired, or weak—as Jesus was during His temptation in the wilderness), staying healthy can shore up defenses against temptation.[4]

CONCLUSION

Singles note feeling frustrated when spiritual growth is encouraged only as a means to an end—to "prepare for marriage." Young singles find this utilitarian mentality especially frustrating because the grow-in-Christ-to-prepare-for-marriage mentality reduces their spiritual growth to one possible outflow. Older singles find it frustrating because as the likelihood for marriage or

> My biggest problem with the way singles are addressed in the church (particularly women) is that every ministry targeted to them has to do with preparing for marriage. Marriage is treated like a given, like a sure thing, like a generic rite of passage that everyone does, like going through puberty. But it isn't. Not everyone will get married. Even some people who want to get married may not get married, or at least may not get married for a long time. And not everyone does want to get married. As a young, single woman in the church, I never go to any of the "Women's Ministries" because they will, inevitably, have to do with preparing to be a wife and a mother, or have to do with "Waiting for Mr. Right," and that is just not a calling I feel is relevant to my life at this point. Where are the Bible studies for women on just being godly women? Or better, just being godly people? Where are the Bible studies on how to honor God in your career, in your leadership, or in your education? It's not that I believe preparing to be a wife is a bad thing; I think it is a very good thing, even a necessary thing. I just wish it wasn't the only thing targeted to young women of my status.
>
> ~ Selina, Single

remarriage dwindles for them, this way of thinking potentially discounts their spiritual contributions.

The response from Selina is representative of many survey takers (especially young women) who expressed similar sentiments.

Jesus instructed His followers regarding what to seek first, and it wasn't a spouse. It was the Kingdom. Our hope for the future is not in a spouse—it is in the Kingdom of God, its people, its purpose, and its promise. True believers live along an everlasting continuum of worship, praise, and adoration: an eternal marriage to the Jesus who loved us and baptized us into the church with His blood.

> The aim of the gospel isn't to be married! The aim of the gospel is our eternal salvation through Christ, regardless of our marital status, as well as our responsibility in sharing the gospel with the world! You don't have to be married to share the love of Jesus! God loves us all, regardless of His plans for us!
>
> ~ Adrian, Married

If the Action Points at the end of each chapter sound time-consuming, that's because they are. If caring for singles sounds as if it requires sacrifice, that's because it does. If this sounds like hard work, that's because it is.

As Christ laid down His life for us, so we lay down our lives for the brethren. Many understand this as a command to care for one another and meet each other's material needs; however, if we nourish the body alone while neglecting the deeper needs of the soul, we only prolong an unsatisfying existence.

By this we know love, that he laid down his life for us,

> *and we ought to lay down our lives for the brothers. But if anyone has the world's goods and sees his brother in need, yet closes his heart against him, how does God's love abide in him? Little children, let us not love in word or talk but in deed and in truth. By this we shall know that we are of the truth and reassure our heart before him; for whenever our heart condemns us, God is greater than our heart, and he knows everything. Beloved, if our heart does not condemn us, we have confidence before God; and whatever we ask we receive from him, because we keep his commandments and do what pleases him. And this is his commandment, that we believe in the name of his Son Jesus Christ and love one another, just as he has commanded us. Whoever keeps his commandments abides in God, and God in him. And by this we know that he abides in us, by the Spirit whom he has given us (I John 3:16-24).*

Acquaintances are incidental. Relationships are intentional. Purposing to support singles in friendship will not only help to fill the emotional gap that many of them experience but will also provide a foundation of mutual trust and respect from which the entire Body of Christ can benefit.

We each see just a small sliver of life through the lens of a limited perspective. Accessing the experiences of others from differing walks can expand our understanding of the world, increase empathy, dismantle prejudice, eliminate false assumptions, and foster growth.

We all need each other. Men need women, women need men, adults need children, children need adults, the strong need the weak, and the weak need the strong. The singles need the marrieds, and the marrieds need the singles.

We all need Jesus.

ACKNOWLEDGMENTS

Flannery O'Connor said: "There is one myth about writers that I have always felt was particularly pernicious and untruthful—the myth of the 'lonely writer,' the myth that writing is a lonely occupation, involving much suffering because, supposedly, the writer exists in a state of sensitivity which cuts him off, or raises him above, or casts him below, the community around him."[1]

Writing this book was certainly not a lonely experience. I had the help of an entire community. Hundreds of Christians from many denominations contributed data and comments through my online survey. Friends, family members, and friends-of-friends stocked my e-mail with clarification and off-the-record responses. Phone calls, personal interviews, Facebook messages, and Twitter comments rounded out the experience. My own pastors weighed in on the project's validity and closely critiqued each chapter. Best of all, church friends leaned over in the middle of sermons to whisper, "*This idea's going into your singleness book, right?*"

In short, it's been a group project from beginning to end. The generous donation of time, advice, correction, and wisdom on the part of every participant has humbled me.

By far the biggest contributor has been the Spirit Himself. Many times, resources and articles would fall into my lap seemingly out of the sky. Friends sent me relevant links or offered book recommendations on the very day I planned to start researching a particular section. It was both humbling and amazing.

Special thanks to Bethany, Jodee, Alissa, and Dawn for brainstorming and for putting up with my endless arm-flailing. You're wonderful friends. Thank you to Pam and Vana for the lunches. Thank you to my parents for looking after my education, both literary and theological. Thank you to pastors Jonn and Jerrill and the leadership of Port Saint Lucie Bible Church for lending encouragement, reading early drafts, and pointing out sketchy sections. Thank you to Nathan for supporting the arts and to Lisa for motivating me to keep submitting. Thank you to my friends, family, and church family for being an amazing support system. I love you guys.

To Marji Laine Clubine and Shirley Crowder, thank you for your careful critiques and wise editorial guidance. The book is stronger for your input.

Most of all, thank you to Jesus for saving a wretch like me.

Any failings in logic, truth, balance, nuance, or discernment have been wholly my own. If (when) they come to light, I beg your pardon.

ABOUT THE AUTHOR

Ruth Buchanan is a Christian freelance writer who holds degrees in ministry and theology. After years of classroom teaching in the United States and overseas, she left education to pursue creative endeavors. She currently produces fiction, non-fiction, and dramas. She's an eager reader, an enthusiastic traveler, and the world's most reluctant runner. Ruth loves Jesus, coffee, family, church, and friends. She lives and works in South Florida. Find her on Twitter: @Ruthette.

If you enjoyed *The Proper Care and Feeding of Singles*, please consider returning to the Amazon page and leaving a comment for the author.

BIBLIOGRAPHY AND WORKS CITED

INTRODUCTION

1. Hillin, Taryn. October 1, 2014. "The Decline Of U.S. Marriage Rates Explained In One Incredible Gif." *The Huffington Post: Weddings*. http://www.huffingtonpost.com/2014/10/01/marriage-rates_n_5915648.html (Accessed 12 September 2015).

2. "5 Reasons Millennials Stay Connected to Church." Barna Group. https://www.barna.org/barna-update/millennials/635-5-reasons-millennials-stay-connected-to-church#.VU4l9_lViko (Accessed 12 September 2015).

3. Moore, Russell. *Onward: Engaging the Culture without Losing the Gospel.* (Nashville: B&H Publishing Group, 2015), 179.

4. Ibid., 60.

CHAPTER 1: "I SEE SINGLE PEOPLE"

1. "Profile America Facts for Features: Unmarried and Single Americans Week: September 19-25, 2010." United States Census Bureau. https://www.census.gov/newsroom/releases/archives/facts_for_features_special_editions/cb10-ff18.html (Accessed 13 July 2015).

2. "Millennials in Adulthood: Dethatched from Institutions, Networked with Friends." March 7, 2014. *Pew Research Center: Social and Demographic Trends.* http://www.pewsocialtrends.org/2014/03/07/millennials-in-adulthood/ (Accessed 5 October 2015).

3. Anzari, Aziz. *Modern Romance*. (New York: Penguin

Press, 2015), 26-32.

4. Snyder, Myriah. "Millennial Marriage Rates Declining." August 8, 2014. *Regular Baptist Press.* http://www.bpnews.net/43127/millennial-marriage-rates-declining (Accessed 6 October 2015).

5. "A Revealing Look at Three Unique Single Adult Populations." Barna Group. https://www.barna.org/barna-update/article/5-barna-update/69-a-revealing-look-at-three-unique-single-adult-populations#.VaQQ4flViko (Accessed 13 July 2015).

6. Hamaker, Sarah. February 29, 2012. "Pew for One: How Is the Church Responding to Growing Number of Singles?" *Christian Post* Church & Ministry. http://www.christianpost.com/news/pew-for-one-how-is-the-church-responding-to-growing-number-of-singles-70586/ (Accessed 13 July 2015).

7. Elliot, Elisabeth. *A Path Through Suffering: Discovering the Relationship Between God's Mercy and Our Pain.* (Grand Rapids: Baker Publishing Group, 1990), 35.

8. Cain, Sian. October 22, 2014. "The Sixth Sense: The Film that Frightened Me Most." *The Guardian.* http://www.theguardian.com/film/filmblog/2014/oct/22/the-sixth-sense-film-frightened-me-most-sian-cain (Accessed 13 July 2015).

9. Moore, 55.

10. Roberts, Donna. "Euclidian and Non-Euclidian Geometry." Regents Exam Prep Center. http://regentsprep.org/regents/math/geometry/gg1/euclidean.htm (Accessed 28 August, 2015).

CHAPTER 2: "WAY TO MAKE IT AWKWARD"

1. Ephesians 4:15
2. I Thessalonians 5:14
3. Romans 15:1
4. Erickson, Millard J. *Christian Theology*. (Grand Rapids: Baker Academic, 1998), 1036-1052.

CHAPTER 3: "TACKED ON"

1. Keller, Timothy. *Preaching: Communicating Faith in an Age of Skepticism.* New York: Viking, 2015, 37.

2. DeYoung, Kevin. February 23, 2012. "Your Theological System Should Tell You How to Exegete." The Gospel Coalition, Inc. http://www.thegospelcoalition.org/blogs/kevindeyoung/2012/02/23/your-theological-system-should-tell-you-how-to-exegete/ (Accessed 17 August 2015).

3. Mohler, R. Albert, Jr. *He Is Not Silent: Preaching in a Postmodern World.* Chicago: Moody Publishers, 2008.

4. Keller, *Preaching*, 181.

5. Paul, Jonn. September 20, 2015. "Nourishing the *Corpus Christi*." Port Saint Lucie Bible Church Media. http://www.pslbiblechurch.org/media.php?pageID=6 (Accessed 21 September 2015).

6. Piper, John. *The Supremacy of God in Preaching.* (Grand Rapids: Baker Books, 1990), 21.

CHAPTER 4: "MIND THE GAP"

1. Colossians 3:16
2. Galatians 6:1
3. Ephesians 4:15
4. James 1:17
5. Kapic, Kelly M. *Embodied Hope: A Theological Meditation on Pain and Suffering.* (Downers Grove: InterVarsity Press, 2017), 24.

CHAPTER 5: "SINGLES ONLY"

1. Stadtmiller, Adam. Summer, 2012. "What Happened to Singles Ministry?" *Christianity Today Leadership Journal* Volume 33, Number 3. http://www.christianitytoday.com/le/2012/summer/singlesministry.html?start=1 (Accessed 12 December 2015).

2. Laitinen, Tim. 16 February, 2012. "The Great Disappearing Singles Ministry." *Crosswalk.Com.* http://www.crosswalk.com/family/singles/the-great-disappearing-singles-ministry.html. (Accessed 12 August 2015).

3. "America: A Nation on the Move." The U.S. Census Bureau. http://blogs.census.gov/2012/12/10/america-a-nation-on-the-move/ (Accessed 14 August 2015).

4. Bonhoeffer, Dietrich. *Life Together: A Discussion of Christian Fellowship.* (New York: Harper & Row Publishers, 1954), 23.

5. Quan Zheng, Ph.D., interview by author, Fort Pierce, FL, 8 September 2015.

6. Tate, Karl. "How Quantum Entanglement Works (Iconograph)." *LiveScience.* http://www.livescience.com/28550-how-quantum-entanglement-works-infographic.html (Accessed 27 August 2015).

7. Halpern, Paul. *Einstein's Dice and Schrodinger's Cat: How Two Great Minds Battled Quantum Randomness to Create a Unified Theory of Physics.* (New York: Pegasus Book Group, 2015).

8. *Invisibilia.* "Entanglement." http://www.npr.org/programs/invisibilia/382451600/entanglement (Accessed 27 August, 2015).

9. Proverbs 15:22; Proverbs 11:14; Ecclesiastes 4:11-12.

10. Keller, *Preaching,* 19.

CHAPTER 6: "WHEN ENOUGH ISN'T ENOUGH"

1. Erickson, 918-919.

2. Sayers, Dorothy. *Letters to a Diminished Church.* (Nashville: Thomas Nelson, 2004), 2.

3. Kapic, 79.

4. Piper, John. *This Momentary Marriage.* This book has been published in its entirety online and can be found at http://document.desiringgod.org/this-momentary-marriage-en.pdf?1439242071 (Accessed 7 September 2015).

CHAPTER 7: "PERCEPTIONS AND MISCONCEPTIONS"

1. Harris, Joshua. *I Kissed Dating Goodbye*. (Colorado Springs: Multnomah Publishers, Inc. 2003).

2. Keller, Timothy. *The Prodigal God: Recovering the Heart of the Christian Faith.* (New York: Riverhead Books, 2008), 42-48.

CHAPTER 8: "WHEN HARRY MET SALLY (AND THE WHOLE CHURCH GOT INVOLVED)"

1. Brennan, Dan. *Sacred Unions, Sacred Passions: Engaging the Mystery of Friendship Between Men and Women.* (Eglin, Illinois: Faith Dance Publishing, 2010.), 23.

2. Ibid., 133.

3. Lewis, C.S. *The Four Loves.* (New York: Harcourt and Brace, 1960), 98-99.

4. Lea, Thomas D., and David Alan Black. *The New Testament: Its Background and Message,* 2ed. (Nashville: B&H Academic, 2003), 411-412.

CHAPTER 10: "THE GOOD, THE BAD, AND THE UGLY"

1. Rayburn, R.S. "Christians, Names of." In *Evangelical Dictionary of Theology*, by Walter A. Elwell, 235. Grand Rapids: Baker Book House, 2001.

2. Dworkin-McDaniel, Norine. January 5, 2011. "Touching Makes You Healthier." *CNN.* *http://www.cnn.com/2011/HEALTH/01/05/touching.makes.you.healthier.health/* (Accessed 19 September 2015).

CHAPTER 11: "WALKING IN A DATELESS WONDERLAND"

1. Feeney, Nolan. March 27, 2014. "Why Selfies Sometimes Look Weird to Their Subjects." *The Atlantic: Health.* http://www.theatlantic.com/health/archive/2014/03/why-selfies-sometimes-look-weird-to-their-subjects/359567/ (Accessed 14 September 2015).

2. Formica, Michael J. May 7, 2010. "Gaining Perspective from Someone Else's Perspective: Look at It From My Point of View." *Psychology Today.* https://www.psychologytoday.com/blog/enlightened-living/201005/gaining-perspective-someone-else-s-perspective (Accessed 12 September 2015).

CHAPTER 12: "ON GIVING ADVICE"

1. Jones, David W. "5 Errors of the Prosperity Gospel." *The Gospel Coalition.* http://www.thegospelcoalition.org/article/5-errors-of-the-prosperity-gospel (Accessed 19 September 2015).

2. Bonhoeffer, 105.

3. An early description of my friendship with Jodee first appeared on my blog, *Catch the Sunshine* in a post titled "How to Make Friends, Part 6 of 7: Listen" (December 8, 2014). http://ruthette.blogspot.com/2014/12/how-to-make-friends-part-6-of-7-listen.html (Accessed 12 September 2015).

4. Dickens, Charles. *A Tale of Two Cities.* Accessed online through Project Gutenberg (Published online November 8, 2004). http://www.gutenberg.org/files/98/98-h/98-h.htm (Accessed 12 September 2015).

CHAPTER 13: "THE SPACE BETWEEN"

1. O'Connor, Flannery. *A Prayer Journal.* (New York: Farrar, Straus and Giroux, 2013), 31.

2. Lewis, C.S. *The Problem of Pain.* (New York: Harper

One, 1996), 149.

3. Piper, John. September 28, 2015. "Sex Belongs to Believers." *Desiring God.* http://www.desiringgod.org/articles/sex-belongs-to-believers (Accessed 28 September 2015).

4. Caine, Kenneth Winston, and Brian Paul Kaufman. *Prayer, Faith, and Healing: Cure Your Body, Heal Your Mind, and Restore Your Soul.* (United States of America: Rodale Inc., 1999), 451.

ACKNOWLEDGEMENTS:

1. O'Connor, Flannery. *Mystery and Manners: Occasional Prose*. Edited by Sally Fitzgerald. (New York: Farrar, Straus & Giroux, 1969), 52.

NOTES ON THE DATA

During 2015, I ran an online survey to collect data from singles, marrieds, and church leaders. I also collected data via personal interviews and e-mail correspondence.

Pastors, elders, and church leaders proved the most elusive responders. Not only do members of this group constitute a fraction of each congregation, but they are also incredibly busy. While I wished for more participation from this group, I'm sympathetic to their time constraints and am grateful for each person who weighed in.

While the sample sizes are imbalanced relative to the actual sizes of the three groups within most congregations, the trends in the data seemed consistent enough to warrant analysis. The numbers were merely a vehicle to frame the discussion, however. The comment section, e-mails, and personal interviews yielded the greatest wisdom and truly shaped the book's message.

SURVEY PARTICIPANTS

Total Respondents: 435
Married: 204
Single: 200
Self-identified Pastors, Elders, Church Leaders: 31

On survey questions regarding church life, the responses were separated among the three groups. On questions regarding personal experience and home life, the third group (pastors, elders, and church leaders) were sorted into their respective groups, single or married.

AGE RANGES

18-20: 10
21-25: 41
26-30: 87
31-35: 77
36-40: 84
41-45: 32
46-50: 26
51-55: 14
56-60: 24
61-65: 18
66-70: 11
70+: 9

OTHER BOOKS BY PIX-N-PENS PUBLISHING

Thank you
for reading our books!

Look for other books
published by

Pix-N-Pens Publishing
www.WriteIntegrity.com

www.ingramcontent.com/pod-product-compliance
Lightning Source LLC
Chambersburg PA
CBHW050115280326
41933CB00010B/1110
* 9 7 8 1 9 4 4 1 2 0 5 0 4 *